Profits in Building Spec Homes

by William A. Maddox

Craftsman Book Company
6058 Corte del Cedro / P.O. Box 6500 / Carlsbad, CA / 92018

This book is dedicated to my daughters Allison, Carrie and Amelia

Library of Congress Cataloging-in-Publication Data

Maddox, William A.
     Profits in building spec homes / by William A. Maddox.
          p. cm.
     Includes index.
     ISBN 0-934041-93-8
     1. House construction--Cost effectiveness.   2. Real estate
investment.   I. Title.
TH4812.M234   1994   94-21808
692--dc20   CIP

Contents

Chapter 1
Monopoly, Tinkertoys and Riverboat Gambling

This book explains how to make a living as a developer of single-family homes. It's written for speculative home builders, or *spec* builders, as they're usually called. If you've considered building a spec home and don't quite know where to start, this manual may be exactly what you need. Even if you're not a spec builder, you will find lots of valuable information here. That's because every homeowner should be concerned with resale value. Every home built will be sold eventually. When that happens, you or your client want the best return possible on the money invested. In a way, every home builder and homeowner is speculating on the value of real estate. That's why this book should be useful to just about anyone planning to buy or build a home.

Spec Builders Are Gamblers

Spec builders match their wits against the housing market, against government regulators, and against changes in the supply of labor and materials. Their goal is to find buyers willing to pay more than the cost of development. That's not easy, and, as I'm sure you understand, it isn't a penny-ante game. Tens of thousands of dollars (plus a good reputation) can be made or lost on a spec home. Taking risks like that isn't for the faint-hearted. Neither is it for the poorly informed. That's the reason for this book. Risk is part of the equation. It can't be eliminated. But every spec builder can *and should* minimize the risk of a financial wipeout. Fortunately, it isn't too hard. This manual will help turn the odds in your favor, recasting what might have been a wild speculation into a well-considered, thoroughly-planned opportunity.

Our focus will be on weighing benefits and costs. It's important that you always weigh the perceived benefit to prospective buyers against the additional cost. Anything that adds more cost than benefit is, obviously, something you should avoid. What you want are things that add more benefit than they cost you. Successful

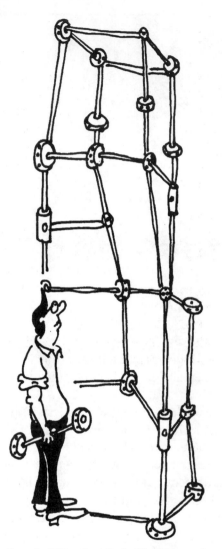

Spec building is a little like Monopoly and a little like Tinkertoys.

spec builders know the value their buyers place on every part of a spec home. That's another way of saying those builders *know their market*. I'm not going to claim that I know the market for spec homes in your area (unless you're building in the Southeast, where I live). I'll admit that I don't know your market. But I do know how to discover what motivates buyers in *any* community. That I'll cover in detail.

Where We're Headed

Starting in the next chapter, I'll take you step by step through the market study and feasibility analysis to land acquisition, home design, financing and construction. When that's done, I'll cover the final step, selling your spec home. Along the way, I'll offer a wealth of practical information, tips and guidelines. To help you organize the acquisition and construction process, I've included several checklists and blank forms. You have our permission to reproduce these on your copier.

Figuring out what *won't* work may be as important as figuring out what will. The market study and feasibility analysis are tools intended to help you make a decision, often before a dime is spent. If you decide to go ahead, this study and analysis become good forecasts of profitability.

The choice of land is perhaps the most critical single decision you'll make. The chapter on land acquisition explains what's important and what's not and suggests how to make the offer. Design considerations are important. Here we'll weigh benefits against costs over and over again. Every design change will affect profitability either for the better or worse. You should understand that effect before making any commitments.

Unless you're independently wealthy, financing is essential. I'll offer what I've learned about getting construction dollars, even when lenders are reluctant to commit on residential projects.

Spec building is a little like Monopoly and a little like Tinkertoys. Monopoly is the planning and financing. Tinkertoys is the actual construction. If you're an experienced contractor or builder, driving nails and pouring concrete may be the most rewarding and exciting part of the process. If you don't have years of experience in construction, concentrate on this part of the book. I'll explain how you can hang on to your profit margin while everyone on and off the site is trying to make money at your expense.

Spec Building Can Be Good Work

I'll admit that spec builders and spec building have their ups and downs. The early 1990s were bad times for many spec builders. Maybe there are times when no one should be building spec homes. But I suspect that the best time to start planning a project is when nearly all spec builders are sitting on their hands. The worst possible time to begin may be when every joker who has two dimes to rub together is planning a spec home. That's the time when you should consider the fast food business or selling shoes — anything but spec home building.

Despite the hard work and occasional frustrations typical of any profession, spec home building can be both exciting and rewarding work. Some people simply seem to enjoy any type of land development — especially where there's the potential for a good profit. I'm one of those who like spec building. I take real pride in creating an attractive, economical home for others to enjoy. When I sell a spec home, I've provided shelter, one of man's three essentials. I've left a legacy, visible evidence of my imagination and hard work. I've developed a well-planned, efficient building that's a credit to the community and a source of pride to the owners. And I've made a buck doing it. That's real satisfaction, in my opinion.

Some Preliminaries

Let me issue a warning before we get too deep into this chapter. Spec building is a complex subject. At first blush, the development (Monopoly) and construction (Tinkertoys) of a single-family house can be an intimidating undertaking. Hundreds of pieces of the puzzle have to come together and fit perfectly before you make a dime. It's easy to lose heart along the way. Every spec builder has plenty to worry about. Unless you were born yesterday, you've seen the headlines:

- Real Estate Market Turns Down

- Interest Rates Soar to New Highs

- Banks Cut Back on Lending

- City Council Passes Moratorium

- Developer Fees Hiked Again

Sometimes it's hard to hold on to your optimism that the project will ever be completed. Maybe the seductive charmer you've created will never attract a suitor.

My advice is simple. It can be done! I've done it hundreds of times. I follow a few simple rules and procedures. I watch the details like a hawk. I take it a step at a time. Simply put, I do what this book describes. And most of the time I make good money. Not always. Nobody does. But I'm still in business, still making a good living and still planning another home. You can probably do as well. At least, you ought to try.

Avoid Early Retirement

It goes without saying, but I'll say it anyhow. There's no point in building a spec home that can't be sold for more than it costs. That's elementary. It's also a point overlooked by more than a few spec builders — many of whom have settled into retirement prematurely. Profit is the bedrock in this business. You have to make profits to survive, to build again, to establish credibility with your buyers, your bank, your subcontractors and the people who depend on you to meet the next mortgage payment. Yet, oddly enough, I've known spec builders who didn't understand the importance of profit, or didn't seem to believe in it, or maybe chose to ignore it.

Despite what may be their popular image, many spec builders aren't motivated solely by the desire to make a profit. Everyone has subtle psychological reasons for doing what they do. Spec builders are no exception. But for spec builders, I believe that eager anticipation of financial gain has to be the primary motivation. Only an intense profit motive provides both the initial desire and staying power to begin a risky project and see it through to successful completion. Maybe that's why some of the most driven, most ambitious, most determined people I know are successful spec builders. No spec home is a simple combination of labor, material, management and capital. Every home is built on someone's conviction that it can be done — and at a profit.

As I've said, spec home building can be both satisfying and profitable. But it's never fun if it's not profitable. People sometimes do foolish things in the real estate business, much as they do around the opposite sex. Objectivity can get lost in the hot pursuit of a major attraction. My advice is to save your emotion for the opposite sex. When you're planning a spec home, be a little hard-hearted. Be objective. Keep your eye on the bottom line.

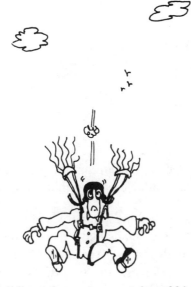

Remember that land doesn't know who owns it. Also remember that unless you're a nationally-known development corporation, the market couldn't care less who's doing the building. You may want to build. You may even *need* to build. But if the figures don't add up, don't do it. Resist the temptation to keep building just to keep crews busy, or for the cash flow, or for the experience. Building a home that can't be sold is like jumping out of an airplane without a parachute. You get a lot of experience on the way down. But who cares after you reach bottom?

Building a home that can't be sold is like jumping out of an airplane without a parachute.

Find Out What's Feasible

Feasibility is a big word. All it means is that something can be done. When it comes to building houses, every house is feasible. Every lot that's big enough could have a house built on it.

But only a fool would try. For our purposes, feasibility means *economically* feasible. It means you make a buck doing it. In this business, sometimes you can and sometimes you can't. Knowing the difference distinguishes success from failure.

It's always possible to lavish money on redwood siding, a shake shingle roof and oak doors embossed with gold leaf. It might even look good and get you some publicity in the Sunday edition of your local paper. But who's going to pay you more than it cost you? Maybe no one. Then you're stuck with a monument to your own foolishness.

Fortunately, there doesn't have to be a contradiction between financial feasibility and aesthetics. All buyers want to love the homes they're buying. That's why you build attractive homes that are easy to love. It's just good business. But that's not your reason for building a spec home. The real reason is to make a decent profit and survive to build again.

Take Your Best Shot Every Time

Generally, I'm going to suggest that you do what's already being done by other spec builders in your community. Avoid pioneering. Once a building is up, it isn't going anywhere. If the market doesn't like what you've built, if you guessed wrong about market trends, you can't move the house somewhere else. You're stuck with a white elephant on the landscape, and red ink on your books.

The market rewards spec builders who are conformist, not innovators. If you want to be eccentric in your private life, go right ahead. The world will be a more interesting place. But understand that eccentric spec builders are as rare as hen's teeth. Play *with* the odds, not against them. Don't take long shots when building spec homes.

My purpose in this chapter is to introduce the major themes you'll find throughout the book. What I've explained so far are the reasons for doing what I recommend in the following chapters. Once you understand the *why* of what we're doing, you'll have less trouble mastering the *what* of doing it.

In the next chapter I'll get down to brass tacks, your *market study*.

Chapter 2
The Market Study

Before we get started with the market study, I want to distinguish a market study from a feasibility analysis, which is discussed in the next chapter. A market study is a way for you to check out the competition. It's like window-shopping; seeing what others have for sale and at what prices. A feasibility study addresses the question of whether you should build or not. It helps you to predict the costs, expenses, income and profit you can expect if you decide to get into the competition by building a spec home. Obviously, you need to complete the market study first. The information you gather is important to the feasibility analysis.

Do It Yourself

I've seen spec builders spend a lot of money on market studies. You could hire an outside consultant and spend thousands of dollars for market research. But you still might not really understand the market in your community. A written report, nicely bound and printed, even if it does place a wealth of information at your fingertips, simply isn't a substitute for seeing what's out there for yourself. As a practical matter, you can't afford to hire this job out anyway. I never rely on others to do this study. I do it myself. Here's why.

First, by looking at houses, asking questions, talking to builders, real estate agents and owners, I get firsthand information loaded with subtle shades of meaning. That's always better than a written report, no matter how complete and comprehensive.

Second, doing a market study isn't that difficult. It doesn't have to be a tedious exercise. You don't have to look at every house being built to understand the market. You just need to look at enough to get a feel for what's available. The conclusions you reach

See what's out there yourself.

on your own, using this data and some common sense, are just as valid as any you could buy. I always feel more confident with data I've collected for myself.

Get a Grip on Your Prejudices

Some spec builders plan homes they would like to own. Often they end up owning those homes longer than they expected — or wanted. That's not why you're in the spec building business. Resist the temptation to follow your whims about location and design. Plan what prospective buyers want, not what *you* would buy. That's another good reason for doing your own market study. It forces you to consider what people are actually buying and what prices they're paying.

Fortunately, it's easy to build homes that are both: what you like and what people will buy. Human needs are more similar than different. If you can't resist following a few of your own prejudices on location and design, combine meeting your needs with meeting the prospective buyers' needs. Just understand that your most urgent need is a profitable sale. The knowledge that your time and money are well invested can make the homes you build look a lot more attractive to you.

Gumshoe your way through the neighborhood.

Taking the First Steps

Begin by determining where it's possible to build single-family homes. Say you've lived in a community for a while. You already have a good idea, from the newspaper, advertising, and from your earlier house-hunting, which areas are the most desirable and active. If you're not familiar with an area, all the necessary information is readily obtainable. All it takes is a couple of sessions of cruising your way through the neighborhoods. Take a leisurely drive up and down the streets. Try to see it through the eyes of a prospective buyer. Focus on the bigger picture. You're aiming for an overview, a sense of the neighborhood. Keep your eyes open and you'll start forming opinions on areas that have potential. Make a few notes if you want. But the most important thing at this stage is for you to get a "feel" for the area.

■ Are there a number of subdivisions under development with encouraging home sales?

■ How many *For Sale* signs do you see posted in front of houses?

■ Is the area on the fringe of expansion and in the path of community growth or is it already established, with little opportunity for new development except in-fill land?

■ Zoning is important too. Is the area zoned for residential or commercial development?

An established neighborhood offers opportunities for in-fill development. There always seem to be some building lots that the larger development companies have overlooked. Eventually, most of these smaller parcels do come on the market. But be cautious here. There's usually some reason why these in-fill parcels haven't already been built on.

Your preliminary drive-by excursions may take a day or more. Take your time. Consider what you see. General impressions are important. Try to see each neighborhood through the eyes of your prospective buyers. Drive back through if you need to refresh your memory. You'll soon begin to form definite opinions about the neighborhoods that show potential and those that don't. Then narrow your search and concentrate on the neighborhoods that are most attractive.

Look at the size and price of houses. Are there completed houses still waiting for a buyer? Look for signs that newly-constructed houses have been for sale for quite a while. Look at the neighborhood as a whole. What sort of condition is it in? Are homes in the area well maintained?

Attending an open house.

Narrowing Your Focus

When you've selected two or three neighborhoods that seem to show good potential, it's time to begin your market study. I like to start with the Sunday newspaper's classified real estate section. It's usually peppered with open house announcements and these are typically broken down by geographic area. Call several of the agents who have listings in the area. If asked, be frank. Tell the agent holding the open house that you're a spec builder and you're doing a market survey. Any conscientious agent will consider you a good potential client. Most will be happy to help you and will pass on to you any information they have on area real estate trends.

Your market survey has to address three issues. I call them the *Where, What* and *When* of spec building:

1) *Where* are homes being built?

2) *What* types and prices of homes are being built?

3) *When* should I build?

When to Build

I consider location (where to build) to be most important. Both location and what to build are key subjects in your market study. But before getting on to these two important questions, I want to devote some space to number 3 —*When to build.*

Timing, Timing, Timing

Deciding when to build always requires some guesswork. It's a function of the local market, the nation's economic cycle, and the world economy. These cycles aren't predictable and don't always move in harmony. For example, suppose the opening of a manufacturing plant has created a mini-boom in your community. Meanwhile, the state economy (or the larger national economy) is going into a slump. Your community may resist the national trend for a while. But take care. A national economy in a blue funk can put a damper on even the most enthusiastic local building frenzy. A local economy won't be able to run against the tide of a weakening national economy for very long. I lost a lot of money learning that lesson.

The opposite isn't necessarily true. A strong national economy won't necessarily help a weak local housing market. Specific neighborhoods have a nasty habit of going their own way even when the economic cycle is strongly positive. And to confuse matters even more, there are usually pockets of home building prosperity even when the home building industry nationwide is approaching extinction.

My own impression is that spec builders stand to lose the most when things are bad, and don't necessarily stand to benefit the most when things are good. Sort of discouraging, isn't it? Now add the time lag between project conception and project completion and the fickle nature of the home-buying public. Will the project still appeal to them by the time it's finished? Put it all together and you have a general idea of the fundamental risks associated with spec building.

Need Some Help?

It doesn't take an economist to determine when to begin a spec house. In fact, I've never met an economist who has made a dime in spec building. Too much knowledge can be a dangerous thing. My advice is to keep your ear to the ground. If you listen carefully, you may hear the distant rumble of economic change.

Figure 2-1 shows one page of a monthly U.S. Department of Commerce publication, *New One-Family Houses Sold.* It shows that in December of 1992 there were less than 285,000 homes for sale. That was about a five-month supply of homes. Compare that with January 1991. We had more than a nine-month supply of homes and new home sales were only 400,000 per year.

You can order a copy of *New One-Family Houses Sold* from:

Superintendent of Documents
U.S. Government Printing Office
Washington, DC 20402

My advice is to keep your ear to the ground.

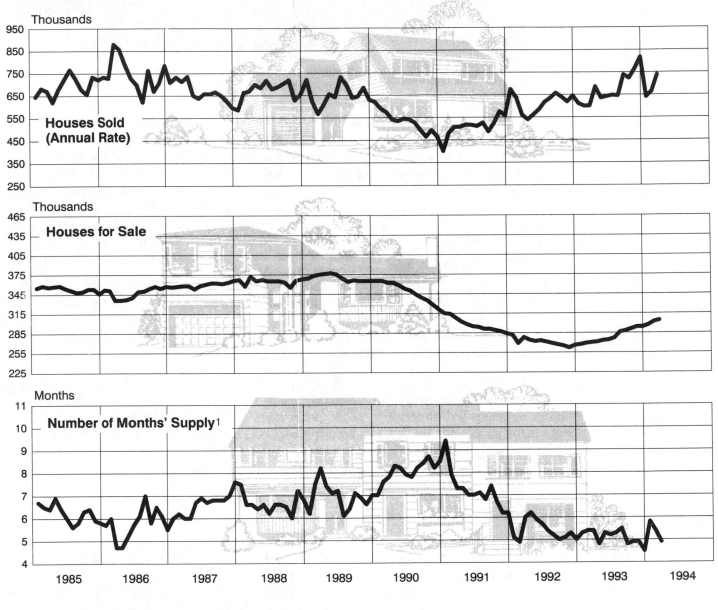

New One-Family Houses Sold and For Sale and Month's Supply at Current Sales Rate
(Seasonally Adjusted)

1   Ratio of houses for sale to houses sold at current sales rate
Source: BUREAU OF THE CENSUS

Figure 2-1   New one-family houses sold

It's safe to say that December of 1992 was a much better time to begin a spec home than January of 1991 — *if you were planning to build in every community in America*. Of course, no one does. There's no national housing market. Instead, there are thousands of local housing markets. Still, publications like *New One-Family Houses Sold* and the predictions of learned economists may be of some help in deciding when to build.

Trust Your Judgment

The truth is that housing deteriorates. Because of that, the stock needs regular replenishing. People have families and families need homes. Somewhere in almost any market there will be some activity. If you know where that market is, it hardly matters what the rest of the world is doing.

Here's your best defense in deciding when to build: Concentrate on what you see with your own eyes, and do the best you can. Then accept the fact that no one knows for certain. You may be sure that three bedroom houses sell best in your market. You may also know exactly where sales are strongest. But you will never be completely certain about when to build. That's a simple fact of life for spec builders and it goes with the territory.

Where to Build

Let's assume you've decided that now is as good a time as any to begin a spec home. You have two decisions left:

1) What to build

2) Where to build

What you build depends, of course, on where you plan to build. So deciding where to build has to be the next step.

Even in a moderate-sized community there will be a number of neighborhoods that offer potential. To decide which of the possible choices is best, you'll have to collect some information in each area. On the pages that follow, you'll find a checklist to help you organize your market survey. Here's how you'll collect this information. Talk with real estate agents. Go to open houses and take the full tour.

"You had to get a home where the buffalo roam!"

Research recently-sold homes, looking for features they share. Pay special attention to the *asking* and the *sold at* prices for each home. Repeat this research for homes currently on the market.

The market will send reasonably clear signals about what is selling and where. Your market study will help decipher these signals. You'll discover, for example, how many bedrooms and bathrooms buyers expect from homes within a given price range. Compare the houses that are selling well with those that aren't. What's the difference?

I've found that information on the single-family housing market is accessible and easily understood. Your best sources will be real estate agents and the multiple listing service, if the community you choose has one. If you latch onto an agent who is a member of the Board of Realtors, you have ready access to both sources. They can get you a printed list of what's for sale and what has sold in the last few months in most neighborhoods.

Use the Market Survey Form

Figure 2-2 is the market survey form. Fill out one of these forms for each home you compare. I call the homes in your survey *comps* for short. Much of the form is self-explanatory. In filling out the form, just make a check mark, insert a number, answer *yes* or *no* or make notes. Be sure to get enough information on paper so it's possible to draw and substantiate conclusions. But keep it simple. There's no need for exquisite detail in your responses here. In fact, too much detail may obscure the essential facts.

Location, Location, Location - Show both the street address and a name for the development or neighborhood, if it has one. If there's no name, you can make one up that will jog your memory later and help you picture the area. Use some natural or manmade feature or boundary that sets off the area as a specific neighborhood. Anything will do, from a shopping mall to a river. The point is to give the area a unique identity.

Source of the Information - This reminds you where you got your information. You collect much of your data simply by talking to people. Recording the source lends some insight as to its credibility. Here are some of the more common sources:

1) Real estate brokers

2) Responses to *For Sale* ads and signs

3) Homeowners

4) Appraisers (Remember, these professionals are paid for the information they have acquired, so don't overstay your welcome.)

5) MLS (Multiple Listing Service)

6) Public records

7) Home Builder's Association (You should join.)

8) Other spec home builders

Market Survey Form

☐ Sold   ☐ For Sale

Location	Date

Street Address

City

Source of Information

Home was Sold ☐   or Home is Offered for Sale ☐   at a price of $

Sq. Ft. heated area	Price per Sq. Ft. $	Year built
Number of bedrooms	Number of bathrooms	Stories
Dining room	Living room	Den/family room
Basement	Garage	Other Rooms

Type of construction ☐ Wood-frame ☐ Masonry ☐ Concrete ☐ Other_____

Architectural style	Exterior finish	Floor finish
Heating	Air conditioning	Fireplace

Appliances   ☐ Oven ☐ Range ☐ Range Hood ☐ Dishwasher ☐ Microwave
☐ Refrigerator ☐ Garbage Disposer ☐ Water Softener ☐ Trash Compactor
☐ Other_____

Utilities   ☐ Gas ☐ Electric ☐ Sewer ☐ Septic tank ☐ Water
☐ Phone ☐ Cable TV

Additional structures

Yard improvements

Special features

Schools

Location considerations

Financing

Comments

Figure 2-2 Market survey form

There's no shortage of information about homes for sale. When approached in a friendly and open manner, most people are willing to answer questions. Just remember that you aren't taking depositions. No one's obligated to help you, but everyone likes to offer an opinion. Anyway, most people in real estate really do enjoy talking shop.

Other spec builders are also a source of information. Most of us realize that the housing market is very large. No one house is going to be a threat to another builder. Most competitors understand this and will be helpful. They may need your help someday and can appreciate your needs.

Every spec builder is or should be researching the market, just as you are. That's why I recommend discussing your own research with the competition. The successful spec builder lives by collecting and trading information, both about opportunities and warning signals.

Sold or For Sale - The distinction is, of course, important. Keep a record of what builders are asking (For Sale). But give more weight to the prices people are actually paying (Sold). While it's much easier to collect the information on the houses for sale, the data on the sold homes is more valuable to you.

The spec house you build will be available some time in the future, not the present. It's normal and healthy when you find houses for sale at higher prices than prior sales. If asking prices are less than sold housing, prices are soft. That's either a distress sign or an indicator of a problem with a particular house. You need to determine which it is.

Price - The Sold or For Sale price.

Number of Bedrooms - Most people use this as an easy way to measure and compare the sizes of houses. Here's how it works. A small house has two bedrooms. A large house has four or more bedrooms. This isn't an accurate or dependable way to look at the size of a house, or to use to compare houses. That's because these numbers can be deceiving. Take an eight-bedroom house, for instance. Perhaps not one of the eight is any bigger than a walk-in closet, but there are indeed eight of them. This is hardly the palatial house that an eight-bedroom house implies in most people's imaginations. This sort of deceptive sizing is why spec builders also consider the house's square footage. We'll discuss how to find and use square footage a little later. Remember, most prospective buyers are thinking in terms of, and shopping for, a house with a certain number of bedrooms.

"As you probably guessed, this is the half bath."

Number of Baths - This is another number that can be deceptive. Comparing this number with the number of bedrooms will provide an indication of how extravagant or frugal the house design is. For example, a two-bath, four-bedroom house is probably skimpy on bathroom capacity. Typically, a four-bedroom home has a minimum of two and a half baths. Three baths would be better. (Any bathroom that has fewer than three fixtures counts as a *half bath*.) Though rarely a negative as a selling point, the number of bathrooms may have a negative impact on the benefit-to-cost equation.

Square Feet - The market for housing is a market for enclosed space. When you can, get the square footage. Your figure should include only heated area. That excludes the garage and the basement, if there is one. Floor area is usually taken to include the width of a typical 2 x 4 stud wall. (Measurements on blueprints follow this practice.) That makes it easy. You can measure the home from the exterior.

Be consistent when measuring floor area. You want to compare apples to apples, not apples to oranges. If you measure one house one way, be sure you measure all of the comps the same way.

Make a note of any unattached or attached structures. This includes such things as overhanging porches, decks or storage sheds. Do not, however, include these in your measurement of the square feet of enclosed space.

Price per Square Foot - Every house is different. Each one's physical condition is different. Each one has a unique location. The home's physical condition, it's general state of repair, is different for each home. Amenities vary and so do neighbors. All homes are unique. You still have to make comparisons. That's why comparing square foot costs is so valuable. The price per square foot is the best way to compare several homes.

The key comparisons in your market study will be the number of bedrooms, number of baths, square feet, price, and price per square foot. But other features have to be considered. Items included in the market survey should help you understand what makes certain homes more or less desirable.

Buyers want more than bedrooms, baths, a kitchen and living area. Every home buyer wants more than simple shelter. They want additional features and usually will pay extra to get it. Within a certain price range, if one house commands a higher price per square foot than its competition, the *extras* probably explain the difference.

Type of Construction and Style - This is where you'll briefly note the home's architectural style (two-story traditional, split-level ranch, three-story Colonial, multilevel modern). Style may be two-story, split-level, traditional, modern, etc. You may also note construction materials used (such as siding).

Appliances - Appliances and built-ins add a lot to the cost of a home. But they also make a home more attractive, not only for their own sake, but because they're part of the (financed) purchase price.

The Neighborhood - Parents with young children are usually concerned about the local public schools. Are the schools a positive selling point or not? This will have a significant effect on the desirability of the neighborhood. Are there parks or green belts nearby? Are other homes in the neighborhood well maintained?

Financing - Did attractive financing, such as an owner carry-back, influence a sale? Be sure you include that fact in your notes.

Other Notes - Under *Comments*, note any other amenities not listed, such as garage door openers, intercom systems, and desirable or undesirable architectural features.

I've found that completing this market survey is the simplest practical means of gathering basic information on the market for existing homes. It collects, on one convenient form, all the critical information you'll need about price and area when you're considering the feasibility of your project. Although you may be tempted to add reams of more detail, resist that impulse. Too much detail can be counterproductive. By the time you study and digest this data, you'll have a much clearer picture of just what your spec home will need to be competitive. Look carefully at other builders' work. Tally up their success or lack of success. All of this helps you develop insight for the market. This is the way you discover how to build the most desirable home for the area. Desirable homes sell for more money and also sell faster. Both of these points are important to spec builders.

How Many Comps?

We haven't discussed the number of comparable homes you should evaluate. That's an important question, of course. My suggestion is to keep collecting information until you have a clear idea of the type of house you would like to build and the price you expect it to sell for. That may not require more than eight or ten comparables. Maybe more, maybe less. No matter how many or how few comps you include in the study, it's a good idea to confirm your conclusions with a real estate agent.

What to Build

Each of the houses you evaluate is probably a reflection of the entire marketplace. As a result, you only need a small number of well-chosen comparables to learn a great deal about your market. Each builder and home buyer has, more or less, done what you're doing. You'll probably discover that in any one neighborhood, most three-bedroom homes with 1,600 square feet built on a 15,000-square-foot lot sell best, and for very nearly the same price. That's the best evidence you'll ever find that you should build a 1,600-square-foot house on a 15,000-square-foot lot — and what you should charge for it.

Before talking to your designer or architect, you may want to add a few more comparables to the study — just to make sure the market hasn't shifted in the last month or so. Once the design is done for the house and contracts awarded, it's too late to make any significant changes.

Meet Ed Kopp, Spec Builder

The best way to explain a market survey is to have you help me make one. I'll get the ball rolling by introducing you to Ed Kopp. Ed's a friend of mine who's about to start his fourth spec home. He's going to let you watch over his shoulder.

Ed got his start in the construction business 15 years ago as an apprentice carpenter, working on his uncle's framing crew. Within five years Ed was running his own carpentry contracting business. By the time Ed was 30, his reputation as a good custom builder and remodeler had spread throughout Tidewater, Virginia. Two years ago, Ed built his first spec home, a three-bedroom colonial in Newport

News. That home sold while still under construction and Ed made a good profit. Last year Ed built and sold two more homes. At the same time, he continued working as a custom home builder and remodeler.

Ed now feels ready to start on his fourth spec home. He wants to try a little larger and nicer home this time. He figures that building a $150,000 house shouldn't take much longer than building a $100,000 house. And the profit margin should be better. Ed's good track record will give him some pull with his banker. Chances are good that Ed's banker will be willing to roll the dice on a larger loan this time.

Over cocktails at the monthly Home Builder's Association meeting, Ed meets Sara Snell, a real estate agent with Happy Homes Realty. As Ed and Sara chat, Sara mentions Mountain Park, an area northeast of the city. She goes on to say that the Happy Homes' branch office in Mountain Park is setting sales records. She tells Ed that Happy Homes is working with several developers in Mountain Park, and in some neighborhoods most of the lots have sold already. However, she says, she knows the other New Hope neighborhoods still have plenty of good lots on the market. Sara also mentions that it's Happy Homes' policy to rebate their commission from the land sale to the builder if he lists the completed house with Happy Homes.

Sara offers to show Ed some good lots in Mountain Park, if he's interested. Ed says he's not sure what's on his schedule next week, but says he'll give Sara a call if he's free. On the drive home, Ed decides to take that first look on his own.

Advantages of Mountain Park

Ed's so busy all through the next week that he doesn't even have time to think about Mountain Park again. Until Sunday morning, that is. Ed, as always, first looks at the real estate section in the newspaper's classified ads. Perfect timing, Ed thinks, as he notes listings for several Mountain Park homes. He's already half-planned a little look-see in Mountain Park when his eye is caught by the open house announcements. Bingo! Three in Mountain Park! Ed's on the road in no time and arrives in Mountain Park well before noon. It's a fine day for a drive and the traffic is light. Ed's got time to get a feel for the area and then stop by the open homes in the afternoon.

Mountain Park is a white-collar, bedroom community. The development's built on some high ground about three miles west of the interstate and about 25 minutes north of the city. Ed finds the three open houses without any problem. Ed also takes note of the other homes on the market. One home is being sold by the owner. Real estate agents have the other homes and two of those are from Happy Homes. One has a SOLD placard attached to the For Sale sign.

Ed starts filling in his market surveys with the data he can gather curbside: address, architectural style, number of stories, and so forth. He can fill in some more details after he visits the open houses, but he knows the fastest route is to enlist Sara's help. She'll be able to call up each home on the MLS computer in her office. He can get most of the information he needs from those files, including the sales price for each home.

After his drive through, Ed decides that most homes in Mountain Park look like they're between 10 and 15 years old. There are also some older, smaller homes, built when the area was still wooded countryside. He's also spotted several newly-built, larger homes, on bigger lots down near the river. Ed also knows, thanks to Sara, that Mountain Park has three new subdivisions currently under development.

Ed quickly finds how right Sara's information is. Some areas really are nearly built out. There aren't many lots offered in Cherokee Hill, the oldest of the three new developments. At the two newer subdivisions, Heatherwood and New Hope, Ed finds there are still large undeveloped areas. Ed counts a total of at least 20 new homes under construction plus 27 lots for sale between the two. Most of the vacant lots, three of the resale homes and several of the homes under construction all have Happy Homes Realty signs posted out front. Well, Ed thinks to himself; Happy Homes certainly is a significant player in this market.

Ed doesn't include either the larger, custom-built homes or the smaller, older homes in his survey. The newer, three- and four-bedroom homes are the ones he wants to know more about. Ed soon finds that nearly all the homes that interest him fit a common profile: single story, two-car garages, full basement, traditional design, total area between 1,400 and 1,900 square feet.

Ed's really pretty impressed with the Mountain Park neighborhoods he's seen. He likes all the signs of the residents' pride of ownership: freshly manicured yards and lawns, well-maintained cars parked in driveways.

After two hours of collecting and recording data on market survey forms, Ed's getting tired. Making a market survey can look easy, but it's tough work. Experience has shown Ed that the choice of a lot is probably the most important single decision he'll make. Time to get out of the car and take a closer look at the open homes.

During the next three hours, Ed stops in at four different open houses (two in New Hope and one each in Cherokee Hill and Heatherwood). At each one, he fills out a market survey and makes a point of chatting with the agent on duty about the housing market. All four agents agree with his own impressions: Mountain Park is a good area and there's a strong demand for housing. The market was down a bit last year, but now that interest rates are looking more stable, houses are really moving well. They all agree with Ed that the best sellers are traditionally-designed, single-story homes with three or four bedrooms, two baths, family room, full basement and two-car garage.

Ed decides to broaden his sample a bit so he stops in at three more open houses. He finds nothing to contradict his earlier fix on the market, so he calls it quits with seven market surveys under his belt. You can read Ed's completed surveys in Figure 2-3.

Before he leaves Mountain Park, Ed drives around some more. This is the way he imprints each neighborhood in his memory. Ed also writes down the phone numbers on For Sale signs posted in some of the vacant lots. Once he's narrowed his search to a single subdivision, he'll come back to check out any new houses that come on the market.

Market Survey Form

☑ Sold   ☐ For Sale

Location New Hope / Mountain Park	Date 24 July 94

Street Address 18 Cottage Circle

City _____

Source of Information MLS - Sold

Home was Sold ☑   or Home is Offered for Sale ☐   at a price of $ 122,500

Sq. Ft. heated area 1418	Price per Sq. Ft. $ 86.39	Year built 1986
Number of bedrooms 3	Number of bathrooms 2	Stories 1
Dining room Yes	Living room No	Den/family room Yes
Basement No	Garage Yes	Other Rooms

Type of construction ☐ Wood-frame   ☑ Masonry   ☐ Concrete   ☐ Other_____

Architectural style Traditional	Exterior finish Brick	Floor finish Carpet
Heating FAG	Air conditioning Yes	Fireplace Yes

Appliances   ☑ Oven   ☑ Range   ☐ Range Hood   ☐ Dishwasher   ☐ Microwave
☐ Refrigerator   ☐ Garbage Disposer   ☐ Water Softener   ☐ Trash Compactor
☐ Other_____

Utilities   ☑ Gas   ☑ Electric   ☐ Sewer   ☑ Septic tank   ☑ Water
☑ Phone   ☑ Cable TV

Additional structures

Yard improvements

Special features

Schools

Location considerations

Financing

Comments Lack of basement probably hurt sale.

Figure 2-3 Completed market survey form

Market Survey Form

☐ Sold   ☑ For Sale

Location New Hope / Mt. Park	Date 24 July 94

Street Address 4326 Rolling Hills Lane

City ——————

Source of Information Open House | Betty Minor | Minor Realty | 555-6132

Home was Sold ☐   or Home is Offered for Sale ☑ at a price of $ 129,800

Sq. Ft. heated area 1478	Price per Sq. Ft. $ 87.82	Year built New
Number of bedrooms 3	Number of bathrooms 2	Stories 1
Dining room Yes	Living room No	Den/family room Yes
Basement Full	Garage Basement	Other Rooms Deck

Type of construction ☑ Wood-frame ☐ Masonry ☐ Concrete ☐ Other_____

Architectural style Traditional	Exterior finish 8" lap	Floor finish Carpet
Heating FAG	Air conditioning Yes	Fireplace Yes

Appliances   ☑ Oven ☑ Range ☑ Range Hood ☑ Dishwasher ☐ Microwave
☐ Refrigerator ☑ Garbage Disposer ☐ Water Softener ☐ Trash Compactor
☐ Other_____

Utilities   ☑ Gas ☑ Electric ☑ Sewer ☐ Septic tank ☑ Water
☑ Phone ☑ Cable TV

Additional structures None

Yard improvements Doll house in back stays

Special features

Schools Mountain Park

Location considerations Good access

Financing Purchasers

Comments Nice Street

Figure 2-3 cont. Completed market survey form

Market Survey Form

☐ Sold   ☑ For Sale

Location New Hope / Mountain Park	Date 24 July 94

Street Address 1823 Indian Valley Rd.

City ——

Source of Information Open House / Jane Davis w/ Happy Homes / 555-2343

Home was Sold ☐   or Home is Offered for Sale ☑ at a price of $ 137,500

Sq. Ft. heated area 1523	Price per Sq. Ft. $ 90.28	Year built 1986
Number of bedrooms 3	Number of bathrooms 2½	Stories 2
Dining room Yes	Living room Yes	Den/family room Yes
Basement ½	Garage Bsmt.	Other Rooms garden rm. off back

Type of construction ☐ Wood-frame ☑ Masonry ☐ Concrete ☐ Other_____

Architectural style Trad.	Exterior finish Brick	Floor finish carpet - hardwood in hall
Heating FAG	Air conditioning Yes	Fireplace Yes

Appliances   ☑ Oven ☑ Range ☑ Range Hood ☑ Dishwasher ☐ Microwave
☑ Refrigerator ☑ Garbage Disposer ☐ Water Softener ☐ Trash Compactor
☐ Other_____

Utilities   ☑ Gas ☑ Electric ☑ Sewer ☐ Septic tank ☑ Water
☑ Phone ☑ Cable TV

Additional structures

Yard improvements

Special features

Schools Mountain Park

Location considerations Nice Street

Financing Purchaser

Comments

Figure 2-3 cont. Completed market survey form

Market Survey Form

☑ Sold   ☐ For Sale

Location New Hope / Mt. Park	Date 24 July 94

Street Address 1726 Indian Valley Rd.

City ———

Source of Information MLS- sold

Home was Sold ☑   or Home is Offered for Sale ☐   at a price of $ 139,500

Sq. Ft. heated area 1598	Price per Sq. Ft. $ 87.30	Year built 1991
Number of bedrooms 3	Number of bathrooms 2	Stories 2
Dining room Yes	Living room No	Den/family room
Basement Full	Garage Bsmt.	Other Rooms

Type of construction ☐ Wood-frame ☑ Masonry ☐ Concrete ☐ Other_____

Architectural style Traditional	Exterior finish 8" lap	Floor finish Carpet
Heating FAG	Air conditioning Yes	Fireplace Yes

Appliances   ☑ Oven ☑ Range ☑ Range Hood ☑ Dishwasher ☐ Microwave
☐ Refrigerator ☑ Garbage Disposer ☐ Water Softener ☐ Trash Compactor
☐ Other_____

Utilities   ☑ Gas ☑ Electric ☑ Sewer ☐ Septic tank ☑ Water
☑ Phone ☑ Cable TV

Additional structures

Yard improvements

Special features

Schools Mt. Park

Location considerations Good

Financing Conventional new loan by purchaser

Comments House looks good from outside

Figure 2-3 cont. Completed market survey form

Market Survey Form

☐ Sold   ☑ For Sale

Location Cherokee Hills / Mt. Park	Date 24 July 94

Street Address 423 Riese Dr.

City ⟶

Source of Information Open House

Home was Sold ☐   or Home is Offered for Sale ☑ at a price of $ 122,500

Sq. Ft. heated area 1525	Price per Sq. Ft. $ 80.33	Year built 1984
Number of bedrooms 3	Number of bathrooms 2	Stories 2
Dining room Yes	Living room No	Den/family room Yes
Basement Partial	Garage Bsmt.	Other Rooms

Type of construction ☑ Wood-frame ☐ Masonry ☐ Concrete ☐ Other_____

Architectural style Traditional	Exterior finish 8" lap	Floor finish Carpet
Heating FAG	Air conditioning Yes	Fireplace Yes

Appliances   ☑ Oven ☑ Range ☐ Range Hood ☑ Dishwasher ☐ Microwave
☐ Refrigerator ☑ Garbage Disposer ☐ Water Softener ☐ Trash Compactor
☐ Other_____

Utilities   ☑ Gas ☑ Electric ☑ Sewer ☐ Septic tank ☑ Water
☑ Phone ☐ Cable TV

Additional structures   none

Yard improvements   Nice yard, owner takes care of it

Special features

Schools Mt. Park

Location considerations Good, though a little further from the Interstate

Financing Purchaser may assume conv. mortgage

Comments
    Older, like most others in area

Figure 2-3 cont. Completed market survey form

Market Survey Form

☐ Sold   ☑ For Sale

Location Heatherwood / Mt. Park		Date 24 July 94
Street Address 1624 Brandywood Ln.		
City ___		
Source of Information Open house / Jim Davis w/ Happy Homes / 555-2343		
Home was Sold ☐ or Home is Offered for Sale ☑ at a price of $ 174,500		
Sq. Ft. heated area about 1850	Price per Sq. Ft. $ 94.32	Year built New
Number of bedrooms 3	Number of bathrooms 2½	Stories 3
Dining room Yes	Living room Yes	Den/family room Yes
Basement Full	Garage Bsmt.	Other Rooms Finished playroom in basement
Type of construction ☐ Wood-frame ☑ Masonry ☐ Concrete ☐ Other_____		
Architectural style Traditional	Exterior finish Brick	Floor finish carpet w/ hardwood in LR/DR
Heating FAG	Air conditioning Yes	Fireplace Yes

Appliances	☑ Oven ☑ Range ☑ Range Hood ☑ Dishwasher ☑ Microwave
	☐ Refrigerator ☑ Garbage Disposer ☐ Water Softener ☑ Trash Compactor
	☐ Other_____

Utilities	☑ Gas ☑ Electric ☑ Sewer ☐ Septic tank ☑ Water
	☑ Phone ☑ Cable TV

Additional structures
Yard improvements
Special features
Schools Mt. Park
Location considerations Good
Financing Purchaser conv.
Comments
Nice upscale house for the area.

Figure 2-3 cont. Completed market survey form

Market Survey Form

☑ Sold   ☐ For Sale

Location Heatherwood / Mt. Park	Date 24 July 94

Street Address 816 Oak Dr.

City ———

Source of Information MLS- sold

Home was Sold ☑   or Home is Offered for Sale ☐   at a price of $ 161,500

Sq. Ft. heated area 1825	Price per Sq. Ft. $ 88.49	Year built 1992
Number of bedrooms 4	Number of bathrooms 2	Stories 2
Dining room Yes	Living room Yes	Den/family room Yes
Basement Full	Garage Bsmt.	Other Rooms

Type of construction ☑ Wood-frame ☐ Masonry ☐ Concrete ☐ Other_____

Architectural style Colonial	Exterior finish 8" lap	Floor finish carpet, some hardwood
Heating FAG	Air conditioning Yes	Fireplace Yes

Appliances ☑ Oven ☑ Range ☑ Range Hood ☑ Dishwasher ☑ Microwave
☐ Refrigerator ☑ Garbage Disposer ☐ Water Softener ☑ Trash Compactor
☐ Other_____

Utilities ☑ Gas ☑ Electric ☑ Sewer ☐ Septic tank ☑ Water
☑ Phone ☐ Cable TV

Additional structures

Yard improvements

Special features

Schools Mt. Park

Location considerations Good

Financing

Comments
Good-looking house, well landscaped

Figure 2-3 cont. Completed market survey form

Ed decides that his next step is to phone Sara Snell. He'll ask her to run a printout of sold houses from both New Hope and Heatherwood. Last but not least, Ed takes down the phone number on the sign at the "For Sale By Owner" house. Ed definitely wants to pay a visit to this homeowner.

On the drive home, Ed reviews Mountain Park's advantages. The neighborhoods certainly look attractive and appealing. Interstate highway access is quick and easy from all three of the new subdivisions. Mountain Park has two large supermarkets, several dozen specialty stores and a multiplex cinema. The new Northgate Mall is just 15 minutes away on the interstate. Every agent Ed chatted with today also noted the high quality of the Mountain Park school system. In fact, one told him that Mountain Park scored in the 90th percentile in statewide exams.

As he's pulling into his driveway, Ed checks the time; only 25 minutes! Ed doesn't like commuting any better than the next guy, so this is a big plus. Most of the drive is on the interstate and Ed won't have to fight heavy traffic. The traffic is all traveling in the opposite direction. Ed's getting more interested in Mountain Park all the time.

Although the housing market isn't as strong as Ed would like, he figures his chances of taking a bath are slim. It's an election year, with the President campaigning hard for a second term. The way Ed sees it, unpleasant economic surprises aren't too likely. Actually, he figures the worst that's likely to happen is that general economic trends all stay flat. On the other hand, the economy just might take a swing upward at the right time. The other major variable is interest rates, and Ed's smart enough to know that he can't predict that.

After considering all the angles carefully, Ed decides he wants to build at Mountain Park. He feels that unless the world comes apart at the seams, a home in Mountain Park should be able to hold its value through economic ups and downs. Certainly it's worth the risk to build one house there on spec. Ed's next job is to narrow down his choice to one of the three new subdivisions.

Prospects at Cherokee Hill

Ed gets to work right after dinner that night. He starts off by reviewing all the market surveys he filled out earlier. First he looks at the Cherokee Hill area. It was attractive, the price range was right, but there really weren't any good lots left. Ed's eyes and instincts told him that the area's built out. His visit hadn't turned up a single good, buildable lot. Every lot he saw had at least one big problem, sometimes more.

The lots Ed saw were hopeless and he knew it. He also knows that scraping the bottom of the barrel only gets you splinters. He decided the best pickings were elsewhere.

Consider Heatherwood

Ed looks at his market surveys from Heatherwood next. There were plenty of good lots for sale there. Ed knows that compared to all the other neighborhoods at Mountain Park, Heatherwood is clearly the best. But the size, price and quality of the homes are a bit more than Ed feels ready to take on. He knows from talking with other builders that home buyers in the $150,000-plus range are more demanding. Ed decides to stay away from these more luxurious homes. He feels more confident and comfortable building modestly priced homes, where he can keep the frills and fuss at a minimum. Besides, Ed's not real sure that his tried and true subs are up to snuff when it comes to the quality and fine workmanship a luxury home requires.

Selecting New Hope

Ed's had a gut feeling all along about the third subdivision. After reviewing the market surveys from New Hope, he decides that it offers the best opportunity for the kind of spec home he wants to build. Homes there are selling in the right price range and plenty of good lots are available. The more-established Cherokee Hill community and the more-pricey Heatherwood neighborhoods are practically next door. However, he needs to collect more information first. He needs to find out what the New Hope lots are going for, and start gathering information on sold comparables.

Bright and early on Monday morning Ed calls Sara Snell at Happy Homes Realty. Ed's an upfront kind of guy, so he briefs Sara on his visit to Mountain Park, his impressions and his decision to take a closer look at possibilities in New Hope. He asks Sara if she'll collect the information on recently sold comps (houses and lots) from the MLS computer. Sara's glad to help, and they make an appointment to meet in Sara's office the next afternoon.

Collecting Hard Data

When Ed arrives, Sara has the computer printouts ready and together they go through the data. Ed is most interested in comparing sales prices, sizes, popular features for best-selling homes, sale dates and overall level of activity. Ed also tries to get a good idea of what the average market life is for homes in the area. In other words, how long does it take for a home to sell after it goes on the market?

The printout gives Ed all the data he needs to complete the "Sold comparables" sections on his market surveys for New Hope. Sara's experience is that new homes don't stay on the market very long in any Mountain Park neighborhood. However, New Hope is still quite a new neighborhood. Very few existing homes have come on the resale market yet. The main turnover comes from military families who transfer in and out in nearly equal numbers. Sara explains that this tends to protect the market prices of newly-constructed homes.

Ed leaves Sara's office more excited than ever at the possibilities at New Hope. On Wednesday he drives straight from work to New Hope to check out the sold comparables from the printout. The list included addresses and sales prices for a total of six that sold during the past year. Ed wants to complete a market survey form for each of them.

Ed finds no one home at the first house he stops at. He doesn't count this as wasted time. He fills in the information he can and plans to drop by again. At the second home he gets really lucky. There's a fellow in the front yard watering the roses. Ed introduces himself as a local builder and strikes up a conversation. Before long, Mike Phillips, the owner, is introducing Ed to his wife, Judy, and their two children. More to the point, though, Ed gets the complete tour, inside and out of the Phillips' home. Mike's really proud he got such a good deal on the house. He tells Ed that a house on the next street with nearly the same floor plan just sold for $5,000 more than he'd paid for his house about a year ago. Mike can't resist adding: ". . . and the lot isn't near as nice." Ed knows that the style and quality of Mike's home are similar to the open houses he saw in New Hope last weekend. He really likes the basic floor plan. With a few minor design changes, it's just what he has in mind.

After he leaves the Phillips' home, Ed drives through New Hope checking out lots with For Sale signs. A gently sloping lot with an attractive copse of mature hardwood trees at the back of the property catches his eye. On the drive home, he decides he'll spend the rest of the evening reviewing his position. If everything checks out, he'll phone Sara about the lot first thing tomorrow morning.

Back at home Ed spreads out all of his market surveys for this project on the kitchen table. First, Ed sets aside all the forms from the Cherokee Hill neighborhood. It's too bad, but there really aren't any lots available that are worth having. For the time being, Ed files the Cherokee Hill data away. He certainly has no regrets about the time he put in on them. They include plenty of helpful background information about Mountain Park. Besides, Ed thinks to himself, a good lot may come back onto the market someday. Anyway Ed's always felt that he puts so much into his completed market surveys that they're not just forms, they're more like trophies.

Next, Ed looks over the Heatherwood market surveys. There are several lots for sale. However, Ed has already decided that this neighborhood is out of his price range for the time being. His instincts tell him that in a few years he'll probably be ready to take on this challenge or one like it. The Heatherwood forms also go into Ed's file cabinet.

Staying on Target

That left only the New Hope forms on the table and Ed pored over them one by one. Reading through the forms, Ed brings up a mental image of each lot and home. He finds the process helps him to round out and interconnect hazy thoughts, plans and ideas. It's how he adds substance and reality to the dry data.

Ed knows from experience that because his focus is tighter now, he often sees trends he missed last time. For example, tonight Ed notices that if he looks at the asking prices in terms of dollars per square foot, they're nearly identical. He soon finds that every single New Hope home sold during the last twelve months went for between $86.00 and $90.00 per square foot. Now Ed has all the information he needs to build exactly the kind of home that he already knows sells best and fastest in New Hope. Here's the formula:

- Architectural style: traditional

- Size: about 1,500 square feet

- Number of stories: 2

- Rooms: three bedrooms, two bathrooms, den/family room, dining room, full basement, two-car garage (located on basement level)

- Other features: fireplace, standard built-in appliances (oven, range, range hood, dishwasher, garbage disposer)

Obviously, the other builders working the subdivision knew a good seller when they saw one. Thinking back to the homes he saw under construction in New Hope, Ed's certain that all of them also fit this profile. That's pretty clear proof that the plan still sells like hotcakes. Contractor's don't stick with a trend for very long once it's lost appeal with the homebuyers. Ed figures there's safety in numbers, so he plans to take the same well-beaten path. Naturally, he wants to add an occasional modest, inexpensive frill to the spec home he builds. Little touches and the right finish treatments add buyer-appeal because they make a home special.

Ed knows there's plenty of time to refine his plans and all the details. He intends to visit any new homes in New Hope that show up in the Sunday classifieds from now on. Strolling through open houses is one of his favorite ways of picking up new design ideas.

Ed's really excited about the project. First thing in the morning, he'll call Sara about that lot in New Hope. The next phase is to open negotiations to buy the land. He's come a long way in just two weeks, and feels confident about the choice he's made.

Reduce Your Risk

Market research isn't nearly as much a mental exercise as it is patient investigation and analysis of the data collected. It's also an essential part of spec building: See the houses. Talk to the sellers, brokers and buyers. Use all the resources available. The most important thing is for you to become as informed as possible. That's the best way to protect yourself. A market survey is a spec builder's homework. *Always do your homework*.

Chapter 3
The Feasibility Analysis

A little like swimming in cold water.

The feasibility analysis brings together in one place all the financial information about the proposed spec home: land cost, development cost, financing cost, construction cost, marketing cost, and sales price. However, there's an even better reason to do a feasibility analysis. It's the best way to get a realistic profit forecast for the project. Armed with this information, you decide whether to go forward with the project, postpone development, or drop it entirely.

Building spec homes is a little like swimming in cold water. You don't jump right in. You test the water first. Doing a feasibility analysis is like dipping your toe in a lake before diving in. If analysis shows prospects to be poor, there's still time to back out at minimum cost and without embarrassment. If the analysis looks good, you ease in deeper. At the same time you commit more of your time and resources.

Think about how much money, time and effort go into building a spec home. The value and importance of a good feasibility analysis should be clear.

Taking Care of Your Best Interests

I feel the best way to look after my business is to stay personally involved in the project every step of the way. I use my feasibility analysis as a yardstick to measure the costs of a project against its potential profitability. I've included a sample feasibility analysis at the end of this chapter. However, a feasibility analysis is more than just a snapshot of project profitability at a given instant. It's a living, growing document that changes as project costs change. By keeping it up-to-date I keep myself fully informed about the progress of the project.

Try to concentrate on the larger numbers.

If you have a computer, I recommend keeping your feasibility analysis on a spreadsheet or word processing program. You'll find it's much easier to make all the necessary changes and revisions on your PC. Naturally, in this chapter, I'll use paper forms.

Whether it's on paper or on a computer, a feasibility analysis gives me a broad view of where the project stands at any point. As the builder/developer, I need confidence in the project's chances for success right from the start. The feasibility analysis provides that. As work continues, I'll rely on many professionals (surveyors, designers, contractors, tradesmen, etc.) to do much of the work of building. But none of them can carry my responsibility for the financial success of the project. I can't delegate that responsibility to anyone. By default, I'm the final judge. My most reliable guide in making these strategic decisions will be my feasibility analysis.

What to Focus On

When I'm estimating costs, I emphasize the large numbers. In other words, the time you spend estimating a cost should be proportionate to the cost's effect on your bottom line. For example, I'd consider it a poor use of my time to labor over an estimate or re-estimating for property tax costs during construction. A 20 percent overestimate or underestimate here won't make much difference in my bottom line. Concentrate instead on all the costs that *really* determine whether or not a project will profit. For instance, land cost, loan interest, and sales cost.

Be Realistic With Your Cost Estimates - It's important to be a little hard-headed when estimating costs. You're planning to spend some serious money. Don't let optimism or fear cloud your judgment. Now is the time to be as realistic as humanly possible. The feasibility analysis should help you avoid underestimating either the time or expense a project requires.

If you don't know the actual cost, lean toward estimates that are probably a little high. Costs are seldom less than what you expected. An estimate that's a bit high adds to your safety margin. Personally, I like a margin of safety that's inversely proportionate to my confidence in the cost estimate. The less confident I feel, the more I tend to pad the estimate. If I overestimate costs and the project is still profitable, no harm's done. However, if higher costs seem to be reducing or eliminating my profit, then I'll review my inflated estimates. Maybe some of the padding can be squeezed out. If not, maybe it's time to back away from the deal.

For some of the items on this form you simply won't know what cost to enter. At least not yet. Don't leave them blank, go with the best estimates available. Later on you'll replace this first guess either with a better estimate or the actual cost. For example, you can't accurately estimate construction costs until you have a complete set of working drawings. That isn't going to happen for quite a while. First you need to close on the land and financing deals. Then the designer has to finish his work. Then, and only then, will you have a complete set of working drawings. Nevertheless, go ahead and make the most informed guess you can. After you've been in the business a while, this gets easier. With a couple of spec houses under your belt, you can base these estimates on previous experience. And believe me, that's a lot easier to do if you keep copies of your feasibility studies. Be sure, if you keep these files on a computer, that you back up the files.

Why Do an Analysis?

I've heard novice spec builders suggest, "This project is a slam dunk. Why bother doing a feasibility analysis?" My answer is simple. I'm never sure what the numbers are until I add up the columns. If doing a feasibility analysis helps me avoid a real surprise only once in my career, then all the hours I've spent doing this paperwork on dozens of projects will have been well invested.

Look at it this way. The risk is major in any spec building project. The cost of eliminating most of that risk is very small. All you need is a good feasibility analysis. Failing to take this step is pure foolishness.

The Feasibility Analysis Form

This form (Figure 3-1) has seven sections:

1) Land Costs

2) Development Costs

3) Construction Costs

4) Financing Costs

5) Marketing & Closing Costs

6) Project Cost Summary

7) Analysis Summary

Don't get discouraged about the amount of data required. There's nothing that's all that complex here. Besides that, it's all information that you'll have to gather sometime in the course of the project. There really isn't a better time than now to do it. The more complete your feasibility analysis is, the more useful it will be to you.

Land Costs

Land costs include the purchase price, closing costs, and costs necessary to get the site ready for construction. Included are off-site improvements (such as utility lines), fees, and on-site improvement costs such as clearing, demolition, retaining walls and drainage lines needed to remedy problems.

Feasibility Analysis

Location _____ Date _____

Street Address _____

City _____

Land Costs

Land purchase price _____

Land closing costs _____

Off-site improvements _____

Demolition & clearing _____

On-site improvements _____

Total land cost _____

Development Costs

Survey & topo maps _____

Percolation test _____

Architectural & design services _____

Engineering fees _____

Soil testing _____

Environmental testing _____

Plan copies & reprints _____

Market & feasibility studies _____

Appraisal fees _____

Insurance _____

Property taxes _____

Legal & accounting _____

Building permits & fees _____

Utility fees _____

Administrative overhead _____

Interest reserve _____

Total development cost _____

Financing Costs

Interest on land _____

Land development loan cost _____

Construction loan fees _____

Construction loan closing costs _____

Construction loan interest _____

Total financing cost _____

Construction Costs

Total construction cost _____

Subtotal Project Costs (due & payable prior to sale)

Total land cost _____

Total development cost _____

Total financing cost _____

Total construction cost _____

Subtotal project costs _____

Marketing & Closing Costs

Sales commissions _____

Advertising _____

Closing costs _____

Other costs paid by seller _____

Total marketing & closing costs _____

Total Project Cost Summary

Land cost _____

Development cost _____

Financing cost _____

Construction cost _____

Marketing & closing costs _____

Total project cost _____

Analysis Summary

Estimated sales price _____

Total project cost (subtract) _____

Net profit _____

Figure 3-1 Feasibility analysis

Land Purchase Price - This is the actual cost or contract price of the land. Exclude everything else. It's helpful for estimating purposes, as well as for future reference, to know exactly what was paid for the land. Keep the land sale price separate from other site improvement costs.

Land Closing Costs - These closing costs include the title report, transfer taxes, prorated property taxes, recording fees and other miscellaneous costs you pay when taking title to the property. A seller may be in default on a loan or may not be able to pay delinquent taxes, liens or the cost of clearing title to the property. A seller may not be able or willing to purchase easements necessary to get access to utilities adjacent to the site. In both of these cases, it's fair for you to request an offsetting reduction in the sales price. If the seller refuses to reduce his price, these costs come out of your pocket and are recorded in this category.

Off-Site Improvements - These are construction costs, but I prefer to list them as land costs. Here's why. Land sold at bargain-basement prices usually comes with bargain-basement problems. The cost of correcting these problems, if the seller won't pay for them, may make the land no bargain at all. I always add the cost of off-site improvements to the purchase price to see the real land cost.

No home can be sold without access to the site or without utilities run to the property line. Getting site access (streets, sidewalks, curbs) and providing utilities (electric, phone, water, gas, sewer, cable TV) is seldom cheap. Land without access and without utilities may seem very cheap. It's probably not. Adding the cost of access and utilities may make the same land very expensive. Part of your challenge as a spec builder is to evaluate the true land cost.

Fortunately, finding the true land cost isn't hard. Just be sure to do it before making an offer or committing to the property. Some sellers will reduce their asking price when they see the estimated cost of getting access and utilities. The building department of the city or county where the land is located will have full information on requirements for access. Go to each of the utility line companies to get information on utility line extension costs. I'll go into more detail on city fees and utility costs later in this chapter.

The advantages to building in an existing subdivision should be obvious. The developer who subdivided the parcel probably had to comply with a subdivision ordinance, providing access and utilities to each parcel. Generally, each lot in a subdivision will already have access and utilities. Still, it's wise to do your own research to be sure of compliance.

Demolition & Clearing - Any existing structures on the site are probably a liability. They must be removed before construction can begin. Demolition could be considered a construction cost, but I prefer to think of it as part of the total land cost. Get a demolition or excavation contractor to give you a quote on any demolition or clearing work that has to be done.

On-Site Improvements - Improvements such as retaining walls and drainage work may be included in construction costs. However, if these improvements are so extensive that they're required

Existing structures are a liability.

before the site can be used, then I include them here. Sites that have good drainage are usually on an incline. Sites like this need a retaining wall if the incline is too steep. Sites on flat land usually don't need a retaining wall, but may have drainage problems. In either case, it's a problem that needs correcting and that adds to your land cost. Get a contractor to give you a quote on any work that has to be done.

Development Costs

These include everything you have to do to get ready for construction. I'll suggest cost estimates in most of these categories. They apply in my area but may be different in yours. Be sure to make your own estimates based on the pricing in your area.

Survey & Topo Maps - Always have a land survey made by a licensed surveyor before closing on the land. The expense is small, usually a few hundred dollars. That's a cheap way to avoid the legal hornet's nest and confusion likely if the lot corners or the size of the parcel aren't where or what you expected.

A survey helps you understand the precise location, corners and boundaries of the property. After the survey is done, get a copy and walk the property. This physical inspection will alert you to problems and opportunities associated with the site. Your architect or designer will use the same survey to draw the site plan.

I feel the seller should pay for this survey. If the seller doesn't agree, try reducing your offer enough to cover the survey cost. In any case, a survey is cheap insurance and the easiest way to be sure of what you're buying. It will also prevent mistakes in siting the house, siting exterior flatwork such as driveways and walkways or siting of other improvements such as fences. It's never fun to find you've built part of the driveway on the neighbor's land. And it's rarely cheap.

Check the survey against the legal description shown on the title policy. The descriptions should be the same. This will verify that what you're buying and what the title policy insures are the same.

If you have a particularly steep site or a site with extreme elevation changes in the area where you intend to build, it might be worth the extra cost to get the surveyor to mark in a few elevation contour lines on his survey map. One contour line every twenty feet is usually fine for most small sites.

The contour lines will help your designer plan both site elevations and drainage. You'll fine-tune the elevation of the building later after initial site clearing and rough grading have been completed.

The survey may be the first hard (out of pocket) cost on your project. Expect to pay between $300 and $1,000 for a survey. Costs are higher if the surveyor has to set new monuments and prepare a corner record for filing with the county surveyor's office.

Percolation Test - If there's no sewer to the property, a septic system will be required. Unfortunately, some types of soil aren't capable of absorbing all the waste liquids generated from a typical home. Under nearly all building ordinances, a percolation test will be required before a permit for a septic sewer system can be issued. A percolation test (*perc test*) will require boring or trenching and analysis by a civil engineer. Estimate a cost of at least $300.

Hire a professional draftsman.

Before scheduling the perc test, be sure there aren't any restrictions that prohibit a septic system on the site. In most communities, septic sewer systems aren't permitted on lots below a certain size. So that's another good reason for obtaining a survey.

Architectural & Design Services - When preparing your market survey, you saw a range of home designs and styles. You should have formed opinions about what was a good design and what wasn't. You probably saw some homes that were an especially good value and had floor plans that were especially effective. Some of the home styles you looked at were probably particularly appealing. I hope you made a list of good ideas that could be incorporated into your spec home. Whether that list is written or just in your head, now is the time to use it. Now, when you're planning the spec home, is the time to put your good design ideas to work.

The home you offer should be the best possible combination of aesthetics, function, efficiency and price. That's your responsibility. You have to define the home to be constructed. But unless you're an experienced draftsman, you'll need to hire a professional to prepare plans that meet your requirements. So your next challenge is to find a designer who can prepare plans for the proposed home.

Construction plans are prepared either by designers (who may or may not be licensed) or by architects and engineers (who are almost certainly licensed). Licensing makes a difference when you apply to have the building permit issued. The plans examiner will usually accept the judgment of a licensed design professional on questions of engineering. The plans examiner may require review by a licensed professional if, for example, the home includes a retaining wall or non-standard loadbearing beams over wall openings.

Most spec builders working in single-home construction do not use the services of an architect. It simply drives the cost up too high. Designers charge much less, but they also provide less. If for some reason you think you may need an architect, consider the costs carefully before continuing on with the project.

An architect's fee for a custom home plan usually is between 15 and 20 percent of the construction cost. To earn that fee, an architect will probably do most or all of the following:

■ Prepare a preliminary design for your approval

■ Arrange for any structural engineering that's required

■ Prepare a final design and written specifications

■ Prepare plans for electrical, plumbing and HVAC work

■ Provide a landscape and irrigation plan

■ Secure the building permit

■ Select the general contractor

■ Administer the contract, including regular site visits

Plans for any civil engineering (such as grading or drainage) would increase the cost.

Home design can be expensive, whether plans are prepared by an architect or a designer. Fortunately, there's an easy way to reduce costs. I usually spend about $400 on a set of plans for a spec home. That's because I seldom design a spec home from scratch. Instead, I adapt an existing plan to the site and make adjustments according to what I feel are current buyer preferences. For most spec homes, there's no need to reinvent the wheel. I use home designs that have been tried, retried and nearly perfected. The designers I work with have an inventory of stock plans and can usually recommend one that (with a few changes) meets my needs. I recommend that you recycle plans the same way I do. There isn't enough profit margin in most spec homes to give up 15 to 20 percent to architectural fees.

We'll go deeper into house design and its effect on project feasibility later in this book. For now, be looking for a designer with a good inventory of house plans whose fees are reasonable. If you don't know a good designer, get a referral from another home builder. Referrals earn goodwill; be sure you tell the designer who referred you.

Engineering Fees - Costs in this category include soil borings and hazardous waste studies. Even if you don't feel these are necessary, they may be required by the lender.

Soil Testing - Soil testing is intended to identify unsuitable soil conditions that might increase the cost of construction or jeopardize the stability of the home. For example, a rock ledge under the surface, a high water table, or pre-existing fill on the site might inflate the cost of footing and foundation work and make construction costs prohibitively expensive.

Real soil testing shouldn't be necessary on most sites. The contractor who excavates for the footings will dig deep enough to get below the frost line and into firm, undisturbed soil. You'll know it when you see it, or you should. The footing contractor should too. The building inspector definitely will. Be sure that you examine the trenches before the inspector shows up. I like to be on the site while excavation for the footings is being done. This is one time when you don't want to skimp. Better to spend a few hundred dollars extra on a deeper footing than to have a building that develops structural problems.

If there are doubts about the soil, or if the lender requires it, you'll need to hire a company to make soil borings. The cost depends on what you're looking for and the type of report that's required. If all you need to know is the soil expansion index, the cost may be only a few hundred dollars. But allow several thousand dollars if you need a report on compacted fill. In most cases, all the lender needs is a few soil borings along foundation lines. The cost for these borings and a summary report should range from $500 to $1,000. If your soil testing company discovers something unusual, the cost could be much higher. If a soil test is required, I like to have the testing

Soil condition that might increase the cost of construction.

done before the land sale closes. A seller who is highly motivated to sell may even be willing to split the cost of the tests.

Environmental Testing - Cleaning up a site that was used to store or dispose of hazardous material may cost many times the price of the land. If it turns out that the pasture you bought was once a toxic waste dump, you can just walk away. The lender's on the hook forever. No lender wants to take that risk. That's why many lenders require a Phase One environmental report before closing a loan on some types of property.

The purpose of an environmental report is to identify potentially hazardous materials that could have contaminated the site. Work like this is usually done by licensed engineers or registered environmental assessors.

A Phase One environmental assessment usually includes the following:

■ A review of government records on properties within one mile of the site. The report will disclose any government record of a release of hazardous materials near the property.

■ A review of historical records at the city or county planning or zoning office. The report will disclose any Environmental Impact Report that has been prepared for land that includes your site, and any petroleum activity within two miles of the site. The assessor will also check local fire department records for any hazardous material permits granted in the area.

■ A review of aerial photographs, past and present, that would show prior uses of the site.

■ A title search going back at least 50 years to show how the land was used by prior owners.

■ A visual inspection of the site and other properties within a mile of the site. The environmental assessor will look for evidence of contamination by hazardous materials, poor waste disposal practice, asbestos-containing materials or PCB compounds.

Assume the cost of a Phase One assessment and written report will be at least $2,500. If the assessment turns up anything unusual, a Phase Two investigation may be necessary and the cost will be much higher. This will come up before you get loan approval and the sale closes. If your lender asks for an environmental assessment, you still have time to back away from the purchase. Consider these costs carefully before committing to the project. It may be better to find another piece of land.

Plan Copies & Reprints - Don't scrimp on blueprints. Be sure there are plenty to go around. Make them freely available to all contractors bidding the job. Having enough copies of the prints will save hours of your time.

Your designer will probably provide one set of pencil drawings on semi-transparent drafting paper. Take your copies from this original. Standard charges for these copies run about $2 for each 2- by 3-foot sheet. I usually estimate a total of eight pages for a full set of plans and specifications. That means each set of copies will cost about $16.

List miscellaneous costs.

Market & Feasibility Studies - This is the place to list miscellaneous costs incurred in doing research for the project. Assume the cost of printing, maps, notebooks, photographs, car mileage and other sundry items will be at least $200.

Appraisal Fees - Your lender will probably require an appraisal. Federally-regulated lenders will require an appraisal by a licensed appraiser. Your mortgage broker or lender will either contact an appraiser (at your expense) or recommend several acceptable (to them) local appraisers for you to contact.

I've heard developers say that the appraisal's quality is irrelevant. They feel that a bad appraisal that gets the loan is better than a good appraisal that doesn't. Good or bad, they claim, an appraisal adds no value to the project. Get the cheapest appraisal you can they say. Better yet, avoid getting any appraisal at all.

I don't agree.

A good appraisal by an experienced appraiser is worth the cost. Any appraiser who routinely appraises single-family houses in the area of your purchase will have access to a great deal of price information. If sale prices are already available, less time will be needed to collect data, and the fee for the appraisal should be lower. With information on hand, the work done should be more reliable, and you'll get a superior job at a better price. That's having your cake and eating it too. It's also an excellent reason to select an experienced appraiser. Here's reason number two:

A good appraisal will confirm the conclusions of your market survey. If the appraiser's value is wildly different from the value you estimated, check your market survey again. Where's the difference? The appraiser may know something you don't. Think of it this way: If the appraiser catches something you've overlooked, it could end up saving you the cost of the appraisal several times over.

Speaking of cost, I usually pay about $350 for a complete appraisal and report. You can expect to pay about the same in most areas.

Insurance - You'll need liability insurance on the house, and coverage for fire, wind or other property damage.

I don't recommend buying theft insurance. Even if available, it's usually not worth the high premium. Insurance companies have discovered that this coverage seems to encourage the tendency of materials to walk off the job site, so they price the coverage accordingly. Instead, self-insure against relatively small losses like these.

Avoid buying too much insurance. Bad things happen more often in imagination than in real life. That sells a lot more insurance than is really necessary. Insurance companies prey on a quirk in the human psyche that emphasizes catastrophic possibilities rather than probable occurrences. Get the highest deductible you can live with. Handle what you can and let the insurance company deal with what you can't. It's a lot cheaper in the long run. If a loss of a thousand or two is going to break you, you shouldn't be in the spec building business. A good share of the profit potential in developing houses is the assumption of risk. The risk of small losses is something you should assume. I feel it's profitable to shoulder considered risk.

Remember that insurance companies are also in a competitive business. Their rates differ and good deals are available. The agent who writes insurance for your home or car may not be competitive in other types of coverage. Get a quote or two for the feasibility analysis. Then get some additional quotes when you're ready to place the coverage.

Property Taxes - Your county assessor has records that show the current property taxes and when those taxes are due. The assessor should also be able to tell you if taxes are current or delinquent on the parcel.

If you're demolishing a building prior to construction, be sure your tax assessor knows it. Property taxes are lower on vacant land. Though your holding period will be short and the prorated taxes small, be on the lookout for opportunities to cut every cost you can.

Legal & Accounting - Most legal and accounting fees will be included as part of the land costs, finance costs or loan closing costs. If you anticipate any other legal or accounting fees, include them here.

Building Permits & Fees - Many cash-strapped cities and counties have discovered the advantages of taxing and regulating all property development. To my way of thinking, I'm performing a genuine public service when I provide attractive new housing at a reasonable price for citizens of a community. Clearly, not everyone agrees, considering the tax and fee burden some communities impose on building.

If taxes and fees where you plan to build have made property development all but impossible, fine. You can build somewhere else. No harm done. Residents of that community will learn to live with what may be the foolishness of their elected officials. The only risk is that you may discover the problem too late, after committing too much time and money to back out gracefully.

My experience is that spec builders and municipal employees are almost completely different personality types. You've got the money and you're ready to take the risks. They've got the authority but prefer to avoid risk. Still, you have to get along.

Working with government employees doesn't have to be torture. When treated courteously, most government employees will respond with courtesy. Remember that the day may come when you need their help or cooperation. At that point, having a history of friendly relations will improve your chances of a satisfactory resolution. There's no advantage to fighting city hall. The only way to keep applications and approvals moving briskly though the bureaucracy is to be courteous, fair and persistent.

Your primary challenge is to find out as early as possible what fees and charges will be imposed. All too often, fees seem to multiply almost by magic just before I apply for the permit. That's why I like to include a contingency allowance in my fee estimate.

Building Department Fees and Charges	
Building permit	$3,221
Plan check	2,093
Earthquake tax	1,011
Microfilm at $1 per sheet	30
Total	**$6,355**
Engineering Fees (based on 1.34 acres)	
Grading permit	$1,100
Major drainage ($5,165 per acre)	6,921
Local drainage ($4,410 per acre)	5,909
Traffic signals ($400 per acre x 6.7)	3,591
Thoroughfare ($400 per acre x 172 x 0.25)	23,480
Total	**$40,569**
Water & Sewer Permits	
Sewer	$6,829
Water, 2" meters	7,960
Total	**$14,789**
Miscellaneous Fees	
Planning fees	$4,600
School fees ($20,430 x 0.26)	5,311
Total	**$9,911**
Total Permits and Fees	**$71,624**

Figure 3-2 Sample city fees

Begin your inquiry about government fees at the building department, engineering department, sanitation department and the planning or zoning department of the county or city where you intend to build. Don't rely on a phone call. Go in person so it's obvious that you're serious. Most of these departments have published fee schedules. Get a copy of the current schedule. Fees are set by a vote of the city council or county supervisors. Ask if there's any current proposal to change the fees. Ask how long the current fee schedule has been in effect. Then ask how the fees will be applied to the property you plan to develop.

Want to hear a horror story? Figure 3-2 shows the development fees for a 60,000 square foot lot owned by a friend of mine in California. The lot was subdivided into eight parcels with homes averaging 2,500 square feet. The estimated cost of construction for the tract was a little over $800,000.

To my way of thinking, these fees are exorbitant. I'd recommend walking away from any community that levied charges like this. Maybe you agree. But my friend in California says California developers pay fees like this routinely. In fact, many communities on the Pacific Coast and in parts of New England have development fees that are just as high or even higher.

You'll notice that fees for this project were nearly 10 percent of the construction cost. Of course, these fees won't necessarily apply where you plan to build. If fees are lower in your community, congratulations! You're the lucky one. But beware! You're also the target. Cities and counties nationwide are taking aim at property developers. They're shifting the burden of providing community improvements to those who seem to have the ability to pay. That's you, my friend, if you build spec homes.

My friend allowed an extra 5 percent for contingency, just to be safe. Unfortunately, that wasn't enough. Fees didn't increase between the time he did the analysis and wrote the check. But conditions changed. Here's how.

There were two additional fees. Checking with the county assessor, my friend discovered nearly $20,000 in bonded debt on the property. This was for sewer improvements and had to be repaid in five years. Payments on this debt had to be made annually with the property taxes. My friend was stuck with a share of the cost for the time he owned the property. That wasn't so bad. But keep reading.

About 100 linear feet of sewer line on this project had to be dedicated to the city before the building department would issue certificates of occupancy and allow utilities to be turned on. Before accepting dedication of the sewer line, the city ran a video camera through the pipe to be sure it was clear, and that it was installed correctly. The camera detected small accumulations of liquid in the sewer line. Apparently the line had settled slightly after construction and wasn't draining completely. The city agreed to accept dedication of the line on condition that a $14,000 cash bond guaranteeing correction of the problem be posted. My friend had to write the check. What else could he do?

Utility Fees - These are deposits or hookup fees paid to the water company, gas company, electric company, etc. before you get access to their service. The costs vary, depending on your area. Off-site improvements to bring utilities to the property line aren't included in this category. The cost of any off-site utility work should be included with the land cost under off-site improvements.

Call each of the utility companies and get a fee quote. Be sure to explain that you're calling about service to new homes. Ask specifically about their requirements for new construction.

Utility companies are as big as some governments, but they aren't government. Generally they're anxious to get new customers. Some may even offer incentives to build certain features into your new homes.

There won't be any competition for water or sewer service. Consequently, people in water companies and sewer departments often don't care whether you use their services or not.

There probably won't be any fee for telephone service. But the phone company will want you to prewire the home for phones. Be sure the wiring cost is included in your electrical bids. Your electrical contractor must follow the phone company's specifications when wiring for phones.

Administrative Overhead - This category includes the little things such as office supplies, telephone, secretarial expense, checking accounts and the like. Even if you work out of your home, calculate overhead expenses as if you were running a business, which, by the way, you are. Try to allocate these expenses by project. That's the only way to be sure how much each project has actually cost you.

Interest Reserve - Even if you're lucky enough to snag a sale prior to completion, there will be an interval of time between completion and closing. Most homes don't sell before completion. Even if the home sells while under construction, there will be a delay between completion and closing. Your lender on the construction loan needs time to validate project completion. That's why you always need some reserve to service the debt on the construction loan.

There's no sure way to estimate the interest reserve required. It's tempting to simply ignore it. After all, who knows what's going to happen? Unfortunately that's not an excuse. Interest piles up quickly on a construction loan.

My rule of thumb is to allow a six-month interest reserve. If you've targeted the market correctly and it hasn't changed too much, selling the house within six months of completing construction should be easy. Some builders doing business in areas where home sales are booming might get by on a three-month reserve, but it would make *me* a little nervous.

Financing Costs

Financing costs include all the fees associated with the construction loan.

Interest on Land - Not all loans are funded by commercial lenders. Sometimes, with a down payment, the seller is willing to take back a purchase money mortgage or deed of trust with the land as collateral.

I strongly advise you against using this method for two reasons.

First, you should never close on the land before you have your construction loan lined up. Here's why. If you close on the land first, what will you do if your construction loan isn't approved? You'll have the land but you won't be able to build on it without a construction loan. Remember you're a spec home builder, not a land speculator.

Second, your construction lender won't accept being the second lien on the property. That means either you'll have to pay off the property mortgage before you can get a construction loan, or you'll have to persuade your construction lender to combine the two loans.

There's only one type of situation where I've used a purchase money mortgage to buy land. That's when I've been in a position where I was buying land far in advance of the time that I knew I'd be building on it. A purchase money mortgage meant that I didn't have to tie up as much of my cash.

Land Development Loan Cost - If off-site and on-site improvements are financed separately or in advance of the construction loan, account for these costs under this heading.

Construction Loan Fees - These fees (such as points and origination fees) are usually a percentage of the total loan amount. Keep these costs separate from other loan costs to underscore the significance of these fees. Keeping these costs in a separate category also makes them available for future reference and negotiation. Lumping these fees with other loan closing costs tends to obscure them.

Construction Loan Closing Costs - These will vary from lender to lender. A list of common closing costs is included in Chapter 7. Not every fee will be assessed on every loan, and some lenders will include other charges. It's best to request a list of costs from your lender or the lender's attorney before committing to a loan. Be sure you know the costs before closing.

Construction Loan Interest - This is interest on the construction loan during the construction period. Obviously, you can't be sure of the exact interest cost. There's no way to anticipate exactly when construction draws will be required or how long construction will take.

Since you can't be sure, and since interest is a major expense, it's prudent to estimate on the high side. Assuming decent weather, reasonably competent subcontractors, timely deliveries and no major problems, actual construction shouldn't take more than four months.

Item	First Month	Second Month	Third Month	Fourth Month
Amount borrowed	$28,125	$28,125	$28,125	$28,125
Total owed	$28,125	$56,250	$84,375	$112,500
Monthly interest	$281.25	$562.50	$843.75	$1,125.00

Figure 3-3 Construction loan interest calculation

Divide the total construction loan by the number of months projected for construction. Use this figure as the first month's draw. Increase this figure by an equal amount each month for the period of construction. Multiply the sum for each month by the annual interest rate and divide by 12 to find the monthly interest cost. Total these monthly amounts to arrive at the total construction loan interest.

Figure 3-3 shows a simple example. It assumes a loan of $112,500, a four month construction period and an interest rate of 12 percent (1 percent per month).

In Figure 3-3 the cumulative interest cost is $2,812.50 at the end of the fourth month ($281.25 + $562.50 + $843.75 + $1,125.00). Notice that this assumes a level monthly construction loan draw. However, if most of the bills come due during the first half of the construction period, your actual interest cost may be a little higher than expected.

Construction Costs

It may not be time yet to get subcontractor bids and material costs tallied, but you should be able to make a rough estimate of construction costs based on the price per square foot. You can change this figure as your information improves. This topic will be covered in depth in Chapter 9.

Subtotal Project Costs (due & payable prior to sale)

This is a *very* important section of your feasibility analysis. As you'll see from the form (Figure 3-1) this section produces a cumulative total. Fill in the totals you already found for the Land Costs, the Development Costs, the Financing Costs and the Construction Costs. Their total represents the costs you must be prepared to cover *before* selling a new spec home.

What does this subtotal tell you about the project's feasibility? A great deal. For starters, can you realistically expect approval of a construction loan for an amount as large or larger than this subtotal? If the answer's yes, then you're sitting pretty. Congratulations! However, if the answer's no, now is the best time to discover this. You certainly don't want this kind of surprise at the eleventh hour!

As a spec builder you need to know if you have the cash to see the project through. If you don't, you need to know how much you're short by. If you're going to see the project through, you need to know how much you need to scrounge up. You don't want to go broke before you're finished. The Subtotal Project Costs tell you just that.

Marketing & Closing Costs

Although most of these costs don't have to be paid until the project is sold, marketing and closing costs are significant. This category includes sales commissions, advertising costs and closing costs.

Sales Commissions - These are the commissions due the listing agent and selling agent when the sale closes. Commission rates on new homes won't go much below 5 percent and shouldn't exceed 6 percent. If a 6 percent commission seems high, it's because you've never tried to sell a home. Marketing real estate is much more demanding than it appears to the casual observer.

My advice is not to agonize over the sales commission. Don't even compare your profit margin with what the real estate agent makes. Just keep in mind that without a sale you're out of business. If a well-paid agent can hasten the process, you've saved interest and anxiety.

Even if you decide to sell the house yourself, plug a 6 percent commission into the feasibility analysis under Sales Commission. Your time isn't free.

Advertising - Your real estate agent will probably pay the advertising cost. If not, list the cost of newspaper advertising, signs, brochures and anything else in your plans for promoting the sale. Faced with the cost of newspaper and other advertising, you may decide to let an agent handle the sale after all.

Closing Costs - Annoying the buyer with too many of these costs could torpedo the sale. So you may be wise to handle some of these costs yourself. Your primary concern is the net cash after closing. A real estate broker or attorney experienced in land sales should be able to supply a list of the usual closing costs. Ask who usually pays most of those, buyer or seller? Then plan to conform to the local practice.

Other Costs Paid by Seller - Occasionally you'll be stuck with costs that are legitimately and morally the purchaser's, not the seller's. Try to avoid them, of course. But if you can anticipate any of these costs, or want to include an allowance for a little bad luck, this is the place to make an estimate.

Project Cost Summary

When your best estimate is listed opposite each of the first five headings on the feasibility analysis form, it's time to total the costs. That's the easy part. The next step is the hardest.

Analysis Summary

Estimating Sales Price - To complete the analysis, you need a realistic estimate of the sales price of the house. This information comes from the market survey that you've already completed. All you need is one figure — the most likely selling price for the house. That should be easy. Unfortunately, it isn't. Pricing is slippery and fickle in the real estate business. There's no way to be sure of the final selling price. Still, you need some dollar figure. Using the information that you gathered in your market study, and your best judgment, you should be able to come up with a fairly good estimate of what your house will sell for. Enter your estimated sales price on the feasibility analysis form.

As I said, no price estimate is 100 percent certain. But if you've completed a market survey on comparable homes, you've done your homework. You're making an informed estimate that will be good enough to forecast the feasibility of the project under current market conditions.

However, your market survey can't predict future prices. That's the risk. Your spec home won't be finished for four to six months. What will prices be then? Obviously, there's no way to be sure what the real estate market will be like in the future. Still, four to six months isn't too far down the road. It's usually a fairly safe bet that prices won't change too drastically during this period.

Net Profit - When you've entered the estimated sales price, subtract the total project cost. The remainder is your net profit. If the profit is negative (a loss) or it isn't adequate return for the time, effort and risk you'd be investing, consider delaying the project until the market is stronger. If the costs are significantly greater than the anticipated sales price, the wisest move is to abandon the project entirely.

To complete the analysis . . .

A word of advice: Don't kid yourself. If the feasibility analysis shows no profit in the job, *don't waste your time.* Go on to something else. Don't build just to stay busy, or just because you've already invested too much time and energy, or because you're too proud to admit it wasn't a good idea after all. There's too much at risk. Spec home builders seldom have a large margin for error. If the projected profit is slim, the best you can do is break even. Imagine what will happen in the worst case. You need at least a 5 percent profit margin as a cushion. Ten percent is better, if you can get it. Otherwise, move on to something else.

It should be clear to you by now that a feasibility analysis is by and large a numbers exercise. Either there's a net profit in the project or there isn't. If the numbers work out, you buy the land and build a spec home on it. If the numbers don't check out you look for another piece of property. Basically, you're building the home on paper before turning the first spadeful of soil. Although this analysis takes time and adds to your paperwork burden, I feel it's time well spent. That's because this analysis is the best way there is to avoid a wipeout in this business. Spec builders deal in risk. But there's no reason you shouldn't do what you can to limit your total risk. The best tool I know that does exactly that is a good feasibility analysis.

The Sample Feasibility Analysis

Let's check back in with my friend Ed Kopp. He's about to reach the point of preparing a feasibility analysis for the spec home he wants to build in the New Hope subdivision at Mountain Park.

Contracting to Purchase the Land

Ed calls Sara at her office the next morning and describes the lot in New Hope that caught his eye. Sara remembers this lot and agrees that it's a good choice. This is Lot 72 and the price is $26,000. Ed says he wants to make an offer on it, and use his standard contingency contract. A meeting is arranged for that afternoon.

Negotiating Price and Terms - At Sara's office that afternoon Ed offers $23,000 for the lot. Sara doubts that the developer will negotiate on the price since it's a good-looking, problem-free lot. However, Sara will give it her best shot. The property developer counters the offer at $25,000. He also agrees to allow Ed six weeks on the contingency. That's not a lot of time for Ed to get all his ducks in a row, but he thinks he can do it. At this point it works to his advantage that New Hope is a new development. Problems with the title or utility access that could really slow Ed down, probably have already been cleared up. Property developers tend to take care of these problems themselves simply because it makes their job, selling land, easier. The developer also agrees to offer two one-month extensions on the contingency for $500 apiece. This extension clause gives Ed the option of buying extra time should he need it. The seller further agrees to give Ed a copy of the current survey for the lot. Ed also knows that he'll get a 10 percent rebate on the cost of the land by listing his finished home with Happy Homes Realty. That means his net cost is only $22,500 ($25,000 - $2,500).

Another Look at the Lot

Ed leaves Sara's office with a signed contract in hand and drives straight to his lot. He has no problem finding the corner stakes, so it's easy to get a good fix on the lot boundaries. Looking over the lot as he's thinking about where to site the home, Ed's also double-checking for any obstruction or problems that might add to his construction costs.

What kind of problems? Here's a classic example: a little rock protruding a few inches above the grade, just about where the house will stand. No problem to lift that out, right? Maybe, maybe not. Is the few inches that you see 50 percent of the entire rock? Or is it 1 percent? Is there a lump of stone bigger than your proposed house lurking down there? It's nice to find this out *before* you pull out your checkbook to buy the land.

Fortunately, Ed sees no problems with his lot. The group of large trees near the back of the lot will be behind the house footprint. The two large trees at the front of the lot won't be in the way of either the house or the driveway. The whole lot is on a gentle slope, back to front and also left to right. This is a site that will never have drainage problems. It's perfect for a home with a full basement and a driveway running parallel to the right property line.

The "First Draft" Feasibility Analysis

Ed arrives home and goes right to work on a feasibility analysis. You'll find a copy of it reproduced here as Figure 3-4. He'll use this first draft to decide whether his figures are in the ball park. If the results are promising, it's time to get hopping. There's a lot of work to finish before he starts building. There's the construction loan to finalize as well as closing on the land and only six weeks to do it all.

Land Costs - Ed's methodical, so he starts filling in blanks at the top and works his way down the sheet.

Land purchase price: $25,000, less the 10 percent rebate which is $2,500. Ed writes in $22,500 on the first line.

Land closing costs: Minimal, Ed figures, probably just the prorated property taxes and the standard recording fees. $200 should more than cover these costs.

Ed's able to skip the next three lines, leaving them all blank. That's not always true, so let's see why he can do this.

Off-site improvements: All the utilities are available on site and the streets and sidewalks are in as well. This is one advantage to building in an established subdivision. In a newer development you may need to make some off-site improvements.

Demolition & clearing: Ed checked on this during his visit to the lot this afternoon. He'll leave all of the trees just as they are. There aren't any rocks or old structures on the lot either.

Feasibility Analysis

Location **Lot 72**   Date **24 July 94**

Street Address **New Hope / Mountain Park**

City **——**

Land Costs

Land purchase price	22,500
Land closing costs	200
Off-site improvements	
Demolition & clearing	
On-site improvements	
Total land cost	22,700

Development Costs

Survey & topo maps	
Percolation test	
Architectural & design services	400
Engineering fees	
Soil testing	
Environmental testing	
Plan copies & reprints	250
Market & feasibility studies	200
Appraisal fees	350
Insurance	200
Property taxes	200
Legal & accounting	
Building permits & fees	450
Utility fees	1,800
Administrative overhead	300
Interest reserve	3,375
Total development cost	7,525

Financing Costs

Interest on land	
Land development loan cost	
Construction loan fees	1,125
Construction loan closing costs	1,125
Construction loan interest	3,000
Total financing cost	5,250

Construction Costs

Total construction cost	79,500

Subtotal Project Costs (due & payable prior to sale)

Total land cost	22,700
Total development cost	7,525
Total financing cost	5,250
Total construction cost	79,500
Subtotal project costs	114,975

Marketing & Closing Costs

Sales commissions	7,500
Advertising	
Closing costs	4,500
Other costs paid by seller	
Total marketing & closing costs	12,000

Total Project Cost Summary

Land cost	22,700
Development cost	7,525
Financing cost	5,250
Construction cost	79,500
Marketing & closing costs	12,000
Total project cost	126,975

Analysis Summary

Estimated sales price	150,000
Total project cost (subtract)	126,975
Net profit	23,025

Figure 3-4 Feasibility analysis

On-site improvements: Ed's double-checked his memory on this point too. The lot doesn't need any grading work. The natural slope is perfect. A couple of hours work with a front loader and the site will be ready for construction to start. The cost for that work goes into the construction costs section.

Total land cost: Ed finds this total comes to $22,700.

Development Costs - Ed's able to skip over the first couple of lines here.

Survey & topo maps: The seller agreed to provide copies of the current survey, and the lot is so regular that a topo map's unnecessary.

Percolation test: The New Hope subdivision lots have sewer service already, so Ed moves on to the next line.

Architectural & design services: Ed fills in $400 opposite this item. He knows what his designer charges because he's worked with him in the past.

Engineering fees: Ed has no reason to expect any special structural or engineering problems, so that's another line he skips.

Soil testing: This afternoon Ed checked the lot for trouble signs and didn't find any. Unless the current survey tells a different story he's safe leaving this line blank.

Environmental testing: Ed knows from Sara that the developer had to have all the required testing completed before New Hope was approved for development. Ed knows he's been saved a major expense here. The seller is mailing Ed copies of the forms that confirm compliance with all the state requirements. He should have these in a couple of days. The title company also will pick up the recorded documents associated with the approval. So Ed skips to the next line down.

Plan copies & reprints: Ed likes to be sure that he has plenty of sets of plans to hand out to everyone who needs them. Past experience tells Ed that 15 sets should be enough. A set of copies usually runs eight pages total, which comes to $16 per set. Ed runs a total, rounds it off to the nearest $50 and enters the total $250.

Market & feasibility studies: Since New Hope is so close, Ed feels a total of $200 covers his gas, mileage and the cost of sundry supplies.

Appraisal fees: Ed doesn't like it but he knows his lender always requires an advance appraisal of the home he plans to build. Then and only then will he open the vaults. Ed knows he's over a barrel here; no appraisal means no construction loan. Luckily for Ed, John Kopple is on his banker's list of approved real estate appraisers. Kopple computerized his operations, does a volume business, has an excellent reputation and the area's most reasonable rates. "Waste of good money," Ed growls, writing $350 on this line.

Insurance: His lender requires a current builder's risk policy and Ed couldn't agree with them more on this point. Ed thinks that any spec builder who'd build without taking out one of these policies has to be a fool. The rates are quite reasonable and $200 will cover Ed's entire cost here.

Property taxes: Ed's only responsible for the prorated portion that matches his term of ownership of the property. The amount owed is calculated and becomes due after Ed closes on the sale of the completed home. Nonetheless it's a cost that will have to be paid, and that's why it's included here. Ed makes a rough guess and enters $200.

Legal & accounting fees: Ed skips this line. This project doesn't have any fancy accounting work and the only legal fees Ed anticipates fall into the section set aside for marketing costs.

Building permits & fees: In Ed's area the building permit fee is equal to one half of 1 percent (or .005) of the total construction costs. Time for a little math. Ed knows from experience that his construction costs tend to average about $53 per square foot. He's planning a 1,500 square foot home. So the building permit fee equals 1,500 SF x $53/SF x 0.005, or $397. Ed rounds that off to an even $400. Now for the other fees, Ed knows there's a $10 street cut fee and probably other fees too, so Ed adds a little cushion to his total. The guesstimate he enters on the form is $450.

Utility fees: These call for a bit more time with the scratch pad, pencil and calculator. Ed knows that his only cost here will be for sewer and water. He skips the water tap charges. He'll have his plumbing subcontractor include those fees in his bid. That leaves Ed with only the sewer impact fees to calculate. The current rate is $200 per fixture.

Ed counts the fixtures room by room, beginning with the two full baths. Together they have a total of six fixtures, since there are three in each bathroom: sink, tub/shower and toilet. The kitchen is next — two more fixtures, one for the sink and a second for the built-in dishwasher. Last, the basement — which adds at least one more fixture for the clothes washer. A grand total of nine fixtures at least. Ed's also thinking about stubbing in for a bath in the basement but he doesn't need to decide yet. Remember that a feasibility analysis isn't carved in stone. Ed knows he'll be changing, updating and refining the data here all the way through the project. Ed settles with nine fixtures for now, at $200 each. That makes his total for this line $1,800.

Administrative overhead: Like many spec builders, Ed's office is at his home. However, that doesn't mean he's free of overhead and expenses in this category; $300 seems about right.

Interest reserve: The new home market in Mountain Park is running at full speed, so Ed feels he's playing it safe with a three-month reserve. This reserve covers the interest cost that occurs after the construction period. A finished spec home sometimes sits empty for awhile. You may be waiting for a buyer or waiting for the sale to close.

In leaner times or if homes in your area aren't selling as fast as in this example, you might be better off staying with the six-month reserve recommended earlier.

Let's get back to Ed and see how he calculates the dollar amount to enter as interest reserve. Ed knows that construction runs four months and he's planning his usual three-month interest reserve. Past experience suggests that the bank will lend 75 percent of the home's appraised market value. The completed home's market value is $150,000, so that's a construction loan of $112,500 ($150,000 x 0.75). Interest rates have stabilized at about 12 percent per annum, or 1 percent per month. So three months' interest on a $112,500 construction loan works out to $3,375 ($112,500 x 0.01 x 3).

Total development cost: In spite of all the lines that Ed left blank, the total he fills in is $7,525. Just $200 here and $300 or $400 there add up fast.

Financing Costs - *Interest on land* and *Land development loan cost:* Ed's not buying a lot that has a mortgage on it. That means he can skip both of these lines.

Construction loan fees: Ed knows that construction loan fees or points in his region currently run 1 percent of the construction loan. Based on previous construction loan closings, he knows that construction loan amount: 1 percent of $112,500 ($112,500 x 0.01) is $1,125.

Construction loan closing costs: Typically, this cost also equals 1 percent of the construction loan. Once more Ed pencils in $1,125.

Construction loan interest: Ed computes this figure using the Construction Loan Interest Calculation shown in Figure 3-3. The answer he finds is $2,812.50, which he rounds upward and enters as $3,000.

Total financing cost: These costs add up to $5,250.

Construction Costs - *Total construction cost:* Ed knows from recent experience that hard construction costs will be about $53 per square foot. 1,500 square feet multiplied by $53 per square foot comes to $79,500.

Subtotal Project Costs - Ed writes in the totals he's already found for land, development, financing and construction costs. He adds them up and enters the result, $114,975. This figure is a total of all the costs Ed must pay *before* selling this new spec home.

Ed already knows that his construction loan isn't likely to be for more than $112,500. Now he also knows that his up-front project costs come to $114,975. The difference between these two figures is $2,550. It's very important for Ed to know about this future situation now.

He has two options to chose between:

1) He goes ahead with the project, arranging some way of covering the shortfall of about $2,500.

2) He ends the project now, cancels the contract for buying the land, and moves on, having lost very little.

Ed knows he can cover the shortfall from his own financial reserves and not feel pinched. The project shows every sign of making a profit large enough to warrant this extra risk. Clearly Ed's better choice is Option 1.

Marketing Costs - Ed won't pay these costs until he sells the home, since they're paid out of the proceeds from the sale. They are, however, still costs of the project, and substantial ones at that. They have a significant effect on the feasibility analysis.

Sales commissions: Ed assumes a sales price of $150,000 for the home. He allows a 5 percent commission and enters the result, $7,500 ($150,000 x 0.05).

Advertising: Ed skips this line. He expects the real estate company to earn that 5 percent commission. The advertising costs are their problem, not his.

Closing costs: Ed knows he can expect these to be between 2 and 3 percent of the total sales price for the home. He opts to use the higher percentage for now and enters $4,500 ($150,000 x 0.03). He has plenty of time to refine this figure later on. For instance, after the final plans are drawn up, and perhaps once more after meeting with Sara and deciding on the final sales price.

Other costs paid by Seller: Ed doesn't anticipate any such costs so he skips over this line.

Total marketing and closing costs: These costs add up to an even $12,000.

Total Project Cost Summary - Ed enters each of the section totals, adds them all up and enters the result, $126,975.

Analysis Summary - Ed subtracts the Total Project Costs from his Estimated Sales Price of $150,000 and the answer is his Net Profit. This works out to $23,025. Not bad. Based on this preliminary projection, Ed was right in assuming that he would make more on the larger house.

Now that Ed's done this "draft" feasibility analysis, he's come up with some starting numbers to work with. At the same time, he's not a guy to fool himself. He knows this is a very rough first guesstimate. There's a lot of work ahead. He knows that as he goes from step to step, these numbers will be changed and refined over and over again.

A preliminary feasibility analysis keeps Ed on track. He now knows where he's going and exactly what he has to do to get there. It's all right there in his feasibility analysis. Ed stores his feasibility analysis on the computer he uses for his bookkeeping. It's a moment's work to change any figure. Then the computer does the rest. That means he's always up-to-date on project feasibility. Were things to change radically for the worse, he'll know it right away. If he needs to back out of the project, he'll have advance warning. Without an updated feasibility analysis lighting his way, Ed (or you) would be blind and groping in the dark.

The Last Word

Finally, let me emphasize that every feasibility analysis should be revised many times before construction actually begins. Update your feasibility analysis regularly as your costs become more certain and you move closer to the decision to go ahead with (or bail out of) the project.

In any case, I recommend being a little conservative in your projections. Plan for a soft housing market. Be a little pessimistic and hope to be surprised. Don't assume the housing market will go into utter collapse, of course. That's not reasonable. Just assume the market will be a little weaker in six months. If the analysis still shows a good potential profit, you're protected. You'll probably come out OK. At worst, you'll break even or recover everything but your time and efforts. If the market improves, if sale prices move higher, you'll no doubt do much better than projected.

Chapter 4
The Development Process

This chapter could logically have been the first in this book. It could also have been the last because it summarizes the entire development sequence — from the beginning (the market survey) to the end (construction). You decide where the chapter belongs. I've put it here to give you the big picture before we get deep in the details in later chapters.

Sometimes there are so many trees that we can't see the forest. Individual trees are like steps in the development process. Just as it takes many trees to make a forest, it takes many steps to complete a spec home. Look at this chapter as the forest. Each tree is important, but in order to visualize the forest you have to understand how all the trees come together. The purpose of this chapter is to give you a wide-angle view of the entire forest.

Getting Organized

My recommendation is that you follow a consistent order when planning and building any spec home. Here's why. There's protection in consistency. Every spec home project offers hundreds (or even thousands) of opportunities for something to go wrong. If you work at random, you're going to forget something or cause extra work for somebody. That means delay and higher costs. Both delay and financial surprises cut into your profit. To maximize the profit available in a spec home, be well-organized and consistent in your procedures. This chapter will help. It includes a detailed list of what has to happen and in what order.

If you've been in construction for a while, you know that a well-organized job is a more efficient job. A more efficient job is a more profitable job.

Even if you have years of construction experience, you may not understand that a well-organized job reduces the risk. There's a good reason for this: Spec builders should never spend money before they have to. Working at random forces you to commit resources prematurely. It reduces (or may even eliminate) your option of bailing out before the construction loan is closed.

Closing of the construction loan is a key event in the building process. After that, you're probably committed to continue to completion. As you advance toward the loan closing date, you should update the feasibility study regularly. You'll have more reliable cost estimates for nearly everything by that time. More reliable estimates make it easier to forecast profitability more accurately. If the cost information you're getting suggests that the project is not going to work, be prepared to drop it. That may not be possible if you've committed too much cash in advance. You may have to abandon several prospective projects before deciding to build. That's much easier if you're not overcommitted.

Each step in the development process should follow satisfactory completion of the previous step. That may delay the project a little because you aren't working on everything simultaneously. But it's far better to lose a little time than it is to rush through a project that can't possibly work.

The Development Schedule

Figure 4-1 identifies the 36 stages or steps I like to follow when developing a spec home. This schedule is arranged to reduce or eliminate as much risk as possible. Sometimes you'll work several steps simultaneously, or even adjust the order. But this basic sequence will apply on most spec building projects. Change it only when your good judgment makes it clear that change is necessary. But avoid changes that increase the risk of loss.

Depending on the circumstances, you may need to add to or delete steps in Figure 4-1. Do so when appropriate. The development schedule is an outline of the development process. It's not intended to cover every possible detail on every job. No list could do that. Still, it should limit your risk of loss and reduce the chance of overlooking something important.

Here are the recommended 36 steps in my development process.

1) *Market study:* This comes first. Even if you've found land that's ripe for development, my advice is to wait until the market study and feasibility analysis forecast a good return on your investment. Just having a piece of land that can be built on is nothing to get excited about. Even the best planned and built spec home is a failure without willing buyers.

2) *Site selection:* Site selection begins when the market study shows adequate demand. You can't go any further until a site has been selected.

The 36 steps.

The Development Schedule

1. ☐ Market study
2. ☐ Site selection
3. ☐ Zoning OK
4. ☐ Sewer or perc test available
5. ☐ Water available
6. ☐ Electricity available
7. ☐ Gas available
8. ☐ Telephone available
9. ☐ Flood plain
10. ☐ Contingency contract on land
11. ☐ Preliminary plot plan
12. ☐ Plot plan OK
13. ☐ Access OK
14. ☐ Title & deed restrictions OK
15. ☐ Review market study
16. ☐ Perc test
17. ☐ Survey
18. ☐ Hazardous waste report

19. ☐ Soils report
20. ☐ Site plan (Storm drainage and grades)
21. ☐ Preliminary building plans
22. ☐ Preliminary construction cost estimate
23. ☐ Feasibility study
24. ☐ Working drawings
25. ☐ Construction bids
26. ☐ Plumbing bids & drawings
27. ☐ Appraisal
28. ☐ Financing package
29. ☐ Financing
30. ☐ Final construction cost estimate
31. ☐ Driveway permit
32. ☐ Building permit
33. ☐ Close on land
34. ☐ Close on construction loan
35. ☐ Contract with subcontractors
36. ☐ Begin construction

Notes:

_____

_____

_____

_____

Figure 4-1 The development schedule

3) *Zoning OK:* After selecting a site, be sure it's zoned properly. Do this before making an offer on the land. Verification of the zoning takes only a phone call or a quick trip to City Hall. Don't waste time negotiating for land that's not zoned properly. Be sure to get a letter that confirms the zoning of your parcel after contracting for the land.

4) *Sewer or perc test available:* While at City Hall, check on the sewer connection. If it's not adjacent to the site, can it be extended to the property at reasonable cost? The cost of sewer connection will affect the price you're willing to pay for the land. So don't make an offer without a firm quote on the utility line connection. If sewer is unavailable but a perc test has been done, get a copy of the test. Be sure the test is still valid.

5) *Water available:* If there was, or is, an existing structure on the property, water is usually available. Check for water meters when inspecting the site. Call the water district office to confirm access to water.

6) *Electricity available:* Normally, power is either available or will be extended to the property at no cost to you. Get a letter guaranteeing service to the site before closing on the land.

7) *Gas available:* If gas is available in your community, it usually reduces the cost of owning a home. Gas heat and hot water in most parts of the country cost about half of what electric would cost. So most buyers prefer gas and are willing to pay more for a home with gas heat. The local gas company will quote a cost for connecting to your spec home. After you have a contract on the land, get a written commitment from the gas company.

8) *Telephone available:* Telephone service is so universal, it's hardly worth checking. But if you anticipate problems, make inquiries. When you call, ask about costs, procedures and how to have service connected.

9) *Flood plain:* Your local building department office should have flood plain maps. See if your site is in the designated flood plain. Your contract with the seller will probably have a clause which guarantees that the property is not in a flood plain. Still, you want to buy land, not a lawsuit. Don't waste time negotiating on any property that's in the flood plain. Most lenders won't lend on flood plain land. Don't show up at the closing ready for action, having lined up financing and paid for a full set of plans, only to find out at the last minute that the property is in fact in a flood plain. There is no quick fix for this and probably no remedy at all. The lender will back out and so should you.

A site in the designated flood plain.

This is a perfect example of the pitfalls that lie in your path. As the builder, you are the point man. It's your money and your responsibility to anticipate all the pitfalls. Ask questions and get answers. Talk is cheap. But ignorance can be both awkward and expensive.

10) *Contingency contract on land:* Your offer for the land should be contingent on certain conditions. There's an example of a contingent purchase agreement in the next chapter. If the conditions aren't met, the sale doesn't close and any deposit you've made should be refunded.

11) *Preliminary plot plan:* Have your designer draw a simple plot plan of the site. This plan should show the lot boundaries, the building footprint and site improvements such as walkways and parking areas. The plan should also show access to public streets and alleys.

The plot plan helps you understand the home size and orientation appropriate for the site. To draw this plan, the designer will need exact lot dimensions and boundaries. Usually the seller's broker can supply this information. If the broker doesn't have a diagram of the lot, check the legal description. If the lot is a simple rectangle, the legal description may have all the information you need. If all else fails, have a survey done.

Most designers charge only a nominal fee or no fee at all for drawing up a plot plan. This is a professional courtesy. And you should understand that it's done with the expectation that you'll hire him to draw up the construction prints when the time comes.

12) *Plot plan OK:* Take the plot plan to the appropriate municipal departments and get their approval. This plot plan will show whether you've complied with setback requirements, parking regulations and zoning ordinances. Revisions are common at this point, so you don't want a full set of drawings yet. If your plan is rejected, do the revisions necessary. If you submit a full set of plans, a turn-down means a lot of work has to be done over. You may have to pay for another set of plans or even abandon the project. Submitting a plot plan first minimizes your risk.

13) *Access OK:* Get the Engineering or Traffic Division to approve ingress and egress to public rights-of-way. Your plot plan and legal description have all the information needed to get approval.

14) *Title and deed restrictions OK:* In some states, warranty deeds are used. A warranty deed includes the seller's promise that you're getting clear title to the property. In other states, sellers provide a trust deed or only a quit claim deed. In that case, the seller doesn't guarantee that you're getting clear title and you will need a title insurance policy. The title insurance investigation provides a history of the property, including past and current owners and any liens or clouds on the title. Generally, you should have title insurance even if you have a warranty deed. Your lender will probably insist on it.

Most title companies will, for a small fee, issue a preliminary title report. Some will issue a binder and waive the charge if the deal falls through. A binder or preliminary title report isn't title insurance, but it will show the name of the current legal owner and any recorded liens on the property. If the title company won't provide a preliminary title report for your use, get your lawyer to request one. Title companies are anxious to work closely with attorneys and are usually happy to respond to their requests.

15) *Review market study:* At this point you're well down my development checklist. But notice this. Your out-of-pocket cost so far has been small. Even if you've paid for an option on the land or had a survey made, your investment is minimal. There's still room to back out without significant loss. From this point on, your pocketbook is going to open wide. So now is a good time to step back and ask some important questions. For example, is it a still good deal? Or is this a good time to reconsider?

Look for flaws in the project — and in your thinking. Think about the land, its location, the plot plan, what you're planning to build and what you know about the market. If you have doubts about the accuracy of the market study, expand your research with additional comparables. New sales data may help you to rethink your project.

The quality of information you gather, and your willingness to take the time to digest and analyze it, should increase in direct proportion to the money at risk. So keep your wits about you as the ante grows.

Order a survey . . .

16) *Perc test:* If no sewer line is available, you'll need to install a septic tank and drainfield. But there's no use going forward if soil conditions are unacceptable. Have a perc test done to determine whether a septic tank system is feasible. Provide the engineer who does the perc test with a copy of the plot plan so he or she knows where to do the test and site the system.

17) *Survey:* If you haven't already ordered a survey, now is the time. You'll need precise information about the physical site. Provisional estimates are unacceptable from here on out. You won't need a topo unless the site presents unique demands.

18) *Hazardous waste report:* If your lender requires a Phase One Environmental Report, now is the time to bite the bullet and have it done.

19) *Soils report:* You probably don't need soil borings unless there's a reason to suspect unusual underground soil conditions. Boring and trenching for the perc test are likely to tip you off to any problems here. Hidden underground soil conditions severe enough to prevent construction of a spec home are rare. But they can happen.

20) *Site plan:* The site plan shows storm drainage, building grades, and parking grades. Think of it as an elaborate plot plan with grades. It helps the designer determine water runoff and establish comfortable grades for flatwork areas such as walkways, landings, parking and driveways. Since the site plan is based on an accurate survey, it reaffirms that setbacks are within zoning requirements.

21) *Preliminary building plans:* These include a site plan, building elevations (exterior views of the building) and interior layout. Your designer will ask for your approval of these plans before drawing the final, and more detailed, working drawings.

22) *Preliminary construction cost estimate:* You can't ask for bids at this stage because you don't have full working drawings. But, since the preliminary building plans show a site plan and building size, you can make a preliminary cost-per-square-foot estimate.

23) *Feasibility study:* Now is the time to update the figures in your feasibility study. You have good estimates of the overhead cost and the construction cost per square foot. With that information, you should be able to make an estimate of the profit potential. Check the bottom line once more before ordering full working drawings. You can still back out before authorizing the designer to begin working drawings.

24) *Working drawings:* These are the final architectural drawings that you will submit for approval to the inspection department. The subcontractors who bid on your plans will use these same plans to do their quantity take-offs and construction estimates.

25) *Construction bids:* When you have final working drawings, distribute them to subcontractors who will be bidding the job.

26) *Plumbing bids and drawings:* Distribute plumbing and electrical plans to the appropriate contractors. It's common in many communities for plumbing and electrical contractors to prepare plans for the work they will do and get those plans approved by the building department. Approval of those plans may be required before a building permit can be issued. In any case, the city or county will be especially interested in any street cuts required to connect gas, electrical or plumbing systems.

27) *Appraisal:* Your lender may require an appraisal before approving the loan. Get a list of appraisers acceptable to the lender and use one you can work with at a reasonable price. Provide the appraiser with copies of your working drawings, the survey and a site plan.

There are "hot-running" appraisers and "cold-running" appraisers. By that, I mean that some appraisers have a reputation for making low appraisals and others have a reputation for higher appraisals. A low-ball appraisal won't improve your chance of getting the loan. So satisfy yourself that the appraiser is a fair and well-qualified professional. Ideally, the appraiser will reach the same conclusions you reached when making the market study. And there's no reason why you can't share the information from your market study with the appraiser. In fact, I recommend it.

28) *Financial package:* Assembling your financial package is a big topic. It's described in detail in Chapter 8.

29) *Financing:* Request loan application forms from the prospective lender and complete those forms. Nearly all the cost information you need to complete these forms will be in the feasibility analysis.

I recommend that you not go any further until the loan has been approved. That could take several weeks, or even longer if the loan committee decides they need more information. All you can do to expedite the process is to provide all information requested as promptly as possible.

30) *Final construction cost estimate:* When price quotations are available from the contractors, plug numbers from the most attractive bids into your feasibility analysis. With a little experience the best bid should be about what you expected to pay, and maybe even less.

31) *Driveway permits:* Your city or county may require approval by the engineering department for any work in the public right of way. Approval of your construction plans by the building department may not include a permit for work in the street or cuts in the curb. If so, you'll have to pay a fee and get plans for street work approved before applying for the building permit.

32) *Building permit:* This is a big moment. Generally, I like to apply for the building permit and deal with the plans examiner. If you worked with the building department and resolved potential problems as the plans were being developed, there should be no surprises. The building permit should be issued promptly, certainly within 30 days.

Many building departments now contract with professional plan-examining companies to do the plan review. I like that because I find it easier to work with employees of a private company than to work with government employees. I suppose these professional plans examiners are paid by the job, not by the hour. Maybe because of that, they have no reason to delay the work or bicker over trivia. Their focus is the same as mine — get the job done as quickly and efficiently as possible.

33) *Close on the land:* This is another real milestone in the project's progress. You've checked and rechecked. You've considered things from every angle. You've summed up so many figures that you feel more like an accountant than a spec builder. You've made projections and estimates on everything that could prevent you from going through with the project. The only thing that could keep you from closing on the deal now is some equivocation by the seller. This is possible, of course, but rarely happens in my experience. By this time the seller has already decided how he or she will spend the proceeds and is probably more anxious to close than you are. Ideally, you should coordinate closing on the land with closing on the construction loan.

34) *Close on the construction loan:* A happy occasion. You should already know the closing costs so there won't be any unwelcome surprises. Usually, closing costs constitute the first draw against the construction loan, so there will be no out-of-pocket expense to you.

35) *Contracts with subcontractors:* If you haven't already done so, nail down final contracts with your subcontractors and material suppliers.

36) *Begin construction: Carpe diem!* - Seize the day!

Chapter 5
Tying Down the Land

It all begins with the land. Although that's not literally true (you should begin with the market study), land is the *sine qua non*, the thing without which you cannot proceed. The entire development process depends on finding available land. Of course, just any old piece of real estate holding the world together won't do. It must be the right land.

The following chapters examine building design, financing, cost estimating and construction — all necessary ingredients. But before making rabbit stew, you have to catch the rabbit. That means contracting for an acceptable parcel of property.

Be extremely careful when selecting residential property. Location is a key consideration. Land is the most expensive single component of most spec home projects. It also has a major influence on the cost of other parts of the job. How the land lays and the grade will have a significant impact on construction costs. The project's success, or lack of it, is cast when you select the land.

Bringing It All Together

Eliminate from consideration all truly unsuitable properties.

As in the first four chapters, I've tried to distill most of what you should get from the chapter into a form to fill out when you're getting ready to make decisions. This chapter is no exception. There are actually two forms that we'll discuss: the land evaluation checklist and, later in the chapter, the contingency agreement.

The Land Evaluation Checklist

Use the land evaluation checklist (Figure 5-1) as a tool to objectively compare several properties when selecting land for a spec home. The checklist will, at the very least, help you eliminate from consideration all of the truly unsuitable properties. This allows you to spend your time concentrating on the properties that *do* have

Land Evaluation Checklist

Location or address _____

City and state _____

Area or major crossroads _____

Legal description _____

Asking price and terms _____

Brokerage Information

Selling agent or broker _____

Address _____

Phone _____

Owner Information

Name _____

Address _____

Phone _____

Property Information

Size of property _____

Lot zoning _____

Annual property taxes _____

Current use of property _____

Any income? _____

Amount due on loans _____ What are the terms? _____

Potential Land Planning Problems

Site configuration _____

Grade _____

Easements _____

Storm drainage _____

Figure 5-1   Land evaluation checklist

Desirable & Undesirable Off-Site Features

Attractive neighboring uses

Unsightly development adjacent to site

Other

Potential Site Planning Opportunities

Lake, river, stream or pond

Attractive, mature trees

Attractive views

Is the site self-advertising (good exposure to traffic)?   Yes ☐   No ☐

Any other outstanding attributes?   Yes ☐   No ☐

How could these attributes be used?

Topography

Is a survey available?   Yes ☐   No ☐

Is a topographical map available?   Yes ☐   No ☐

Type of soil

Is a soils report available?

How much earth fill and compaction will be required?

Estimate of increased foundation costs due to topography

Land Area Required For

Vertical slope

Flood area

Unusual site configurations

Setbacks and easements

Existing Physical Improvements

Approximate value

Condition of improvements

Can improvements be utilized?

Is demolition necessary?   Yes ☐   No ☐   Cost

Figure 5-1 (cont.)   Land evaluation checklist

Possible Constraints on Property Value

Flood risk   Yes ☐   No ☐   Explain _____

Poor drainage   Yes ☐   No ☐   Explain _____

Earthquake   Yes ☐   No ☐   Explain _____

Unsightly view   Yes ☐   No ☐   Explain _____

Noise   Yes ☐   No ☐   Explain _____

Fire hazard   Yes ☐   No ☐   Explain _____

Slide danger   Yes ☐   No ☐   Explain _____

Excess road traffic Yes ☐   No ☐   Explain _____

Excess air traffic Yes ☐   No ☐   Explain _____

Other   Yes ☐   No ☐   Explain _____

Government Restrictions and Burdens on Development

Deed restrictions

Zoning variance required?   Yes ☐   No ☐   To what zone

Setback requirements   Front   Side   Rear

Height limits

Lot coverage restrictions

Parking requirements

Sign restrictions

Landscaping ordinance

Any liens or bonded debt on the property   Yes ☐   No ☐   How much?

Developer fees anticipated

Other restrictions that will affect development

Driving Time or Distance to Community Facilities

Commercial hub

Employment centers

Airport

Figure 5-1 (cont.)   Land evaluation checklist

Entertainment _____

Freeway or expressway _____

Major intersection _____

Elementary school _____

Secondary school _____

Bus service or public transportation _____

Roadway Access

Property is on a ☐ Private road ☐ Paved public road

Any costs to acquire or improve access? Yes ☐ No ☐

If private road, is access to the property guaranteed? Yes ☐ No ☐

Any proposed highway plans that would affect property? Yes ☐ No ☐

Gas Service

Gas line on site Yes ☐ No ☐ Length of run _____

Size of gas line _____ Cost to extend _____

Any problems with use? _____ Service fee ___

Electric Service

Electric line on site Yes ☐ No ☐ Length of run _____

Must relocate? _____ Go underground off site? __

Cost of run to panel _____ Any problems with use? ___

Service fee _____

Water Service

Water line on site Yes ☐ No ☐ Length of run _____

Pressure _____ Cost to extend _____

Any problems with use? _____

Water furnished by _____

Is service fee refunded to the developer? Yes ☐ No ☐ Service fee _____

Refund formula _____

Water well required? Yes ☐ No ☐

Figure 5-1 (cont.) Land evaluation checklist

Well depth _____ Capacity _____

Any problems with well water use? _____

Sewer Service

Sewer line adjacent to the site?   Yes ☐   No ☐   Length of run _____

Size _____ Depth _____ Cost to extend _____

Service fee _____

Will pumping station be required?   Yes ☐   No ☐   Cost _____

Perc test available?   Yes ☐   No ☐   When performed _____

Comparative Evaluation

Is property higher or lower in price than sold comparables? _____

Reasons for higher or lower price _____

Can value be added by

Creative financing   Yes ☐   No ☐   Explain _____

Land planning   Yes ☐   No ☐   Explain _____

Subdivision   Yes ☐   No ☐   Explain _____

Rezoning   Yes ☐   No ☐   Explain _____

Financial Considerations

How long can you afford to hold the land before development? _____

What are the annual holding costs? _____

All considered, what would be a reasonable price for the property? _____

Financial outlook _____

Local bank advice _____

Local savings and loan advice _____

Local mortgage broker-banker advice _____

Lender's opinion of area _____

Lender's opinion of site _____

Will lender make loan commitment on project? _____

Terms offered by lender _____

Figure 5-1 (cont.)   Land evaluation checklist

Detatched Housing Market

What sales price can be expected based on sales price of comparable houses?

What holding period can be expected based on comparable projects?

Is the area over-built?   Yes ☐   No ☐   Under-built?   Yes ☐   No ☐

Will the area be over-built a year from now?   Yes ☐   No ☐

Is the market for detached housing   ☐ improving   ☐ deteriorating

Profit Margin

What is the most likely sales price?   _____

What is the estimated total development cost?   _____

What is the anticipated dollar profit?   _____

What is the dollar profit as a percentage of investment?   _____

Figure 5-1 (cont.)   Land evaluation checklist

real promise. Of course, no checklist can cover all the subjective criteria that make one parcel more or less valuable than another. The information covered in Figure 5-1 may be all the data you need. If not, at least it will serve as a starting point for further inquiry. In any case, this form is the launching pad for further analysis covered in the feasibility analysis and development schedule.

The land evaluation checklist is very comprehensive. Glance over it now. Then use it later as a checklist for the points you want to consider when selecting any property. Simply check off the items or make a note beside the item showing that you've either verified the item or that you feel comfortable with it. Think of this checklist as a shield against major surprises later on that could inflate your development costs or reduce the value of the completed project.

The land evaluation checklist is largely self-explanatory. But there are a few items I'd like to clarify and explain.

Location or address: If you have an address, good. If not, identify the lot's location somehow. Location might be something like:

> *The lot west of the yellow and green house on Chestnut Road.*

Area or major crossroads: Generally you'll want to make all your comparisons within a single neighborhood. The area may be the name of the surrounding development or the name you'll use to remember the parcel.

Legal description: The identifier (such as lot and block number) that appears on the deed and property tax bill.

Potential Land Planning Problems - Under this category you'll make notes on problems that may affect building on the site, such as a huge boulder sitting right where the house will be sited or a drainage ditch running through the back of the lot. Also cover anything about the neighborhood and immediate neighbors that you may want to remember. Consider why this particular lot has been left undeveloped. Write down anything that might be useful in evaluating the property or in comparing it with other properties. Road access, sewer and utilities are covered later in the form.

Site configuration: Is the lot irregular or does it have any physical characteristics that may make building difficult? Make a rough sketch of the lot on the back of the form to help you remember what you see.

Grade: Any site with a grade of over 10 percent is more expensive to build on. Steeper sites will have higher costs for foundations, retaining walls and driveways. Plus, construction is more difficult and takes longer on hillsides. In wet weather, steep sites tend to suffer more from erosion. They also have a higher risk of subsidence. Even after the home is completed, a steep site may be considered undesirable by older home buyers or buyers with young children. You want your home to appeal to as broad a population of buyers as possible.

Any grade over 10 percent is more expensive . . .

The advantage of steeper sites is that the view may be better. That may make the lot much more valuable to some buyers. But be sure to weigh the potential premium of a view lot against the higher construction costs associated with a steep site.

However, just because a steep site is less desirable, don't assume that the ideal site is perfectly flat. It isn't. A gradual slope provides better natural drainage.

Easements: Is the lot used as a point of access to another property, stream, lake or beach? Are there easements other than standard utility easements that may limit usable building area?

Desirable & Undesirable Off-Site Features - This is the place for points you may want to keep in mind about special neighborhood features. Good and bad points are separated so they're easier to weigh against each other, almost at a glance.

Desirable off-site features include a category I've called "attractive neighboring uses." This includes such things as greenbelts or open space, public parks, libraries, recreational facilities, and proximity to schools and shopping.

Undesirable off-site features includes a category I've called "unsightly development adjacent to site." These are problems that might prompt people to buy elsewhere. They include such things as a run-down house or houses nearby, an unsightly view, close proximity to a commercial/industrial area, or a sewage treatment plant or other facility that may produce foul odors or excessive noise in the area.

Negotiating the Deal

When you're satisfied that the parcel is acceptable, it's time to make an offer. This isn't a book on negotiation, but I'll suggest several approaches that have worked for me many times.

A friend who's a trial attorney told me once that he never asks a question of a witness if he doesn't already know the answer. That's also a good rule of negotiation. Don't make an offer until you know what the parcel is really worth. You can't know that until you've done some comparing and checking. Just as a trial attorney has to know the answer before he asks the question, you have to know the true value before you make an offer. You'd sure hate to offer $100,000, have the offer accepted, and then find out it's only worth $80,000.

Occasionally you may be able to "steal" a parcel at a below-market price. But land sold at bargain basement prices isn't always a good value. Before stealing anything, be sure it's worth stealing. If you're getting a deal that's too good to be true, there's probably a reason. That's why I prefer to begin negotiating from the market price, not the seller's asking price.

Don't assume that the owner knows what the property is worth. Figure out for yourself what the land is worth. Then make an offer based on that figure. Not surprisingly, most owners err on the high side when valuing their holdings. It's a mistake to make an offer based on a percentage of the owner's asking price rather than your evaluation of market value. Don't assume, for example, that if the owner is asking $100,000, you should offer a flat 5 or 10 percent less. In doing that, you might still end up overpaying.

It can happen that your valuation is higher than the seller's asking price. In this unlikely event go with the seller's price, or offer less, but be sure you haven't missed anything. The seller may be considering something you haven't.

An Offer Based on Comparables

To make an offer based on market value, you need good information on selling prices of comparable property. You have to do some homework. Of course, this homework pays a lot better than the homework you did in school.

I've already suggested that you collect information on the sale of comparable parcels. This is the time to use that information. Concentrate on parcels that have sold recently, within the last six months.

THE BUYER   THE SELLER

Don't assume that the owner knows what the property is worth.

As explained earlier, appraisers, landowners, other builders and real estate agents have access to sale prices on comparable properties. But these aren't the only good sources. Your county recorder's office probably collects information on purchase prices. Most counties levy a tax or recording fee on property transactions. This tax is usually based on the selling price. In some counties, stamps affixed to the recorded instrument show the stated value of the transaction. Sometimes a stated value is listed when the deed is recorded. Of course, the value claimed may not be actual cash price. Both seller and buyer may have reasons to obscure the true cost. But if the stated value makes sense, it's probably a legitimate sale price.

If the buyer is assuming a loan on the property, the amount of the loan may not be reflected in the sales price. For example, if a buyer is paying $100,000 and assuming a loan for another $100,000, the fee may be based on the amount actually changing hands ($100,000) rather than the full value ($200,000). If the reported sales price varies too much from the norm, try to find out why. Call the seller, purchaser or closing attorney to confirm the sale price. Sometimes it takes a bit of detective work to be sure you've got reliable information.

While you're at the recorder's office researching selling prices, do a little research on the parcel you plan to buy. Find out how much the current owner paid for that land and when the transaction took place. That's valuable information when you're negotiating the price.

Snooping through county records won't help establish comparable values until you know something about the property bought and sold. The deed probably doesn't show the square footage and certainly won't say anything about grade, the view, or the utilities available. To get that information, you'll have to inspect the property.

I'm always willing to disclose the information I collect about comparables when negotiating to buy a parcel. But I won't disclose what I feel the property is worth to me — the money to be made once I've developed and sold the property. That's my little secret. And if things work out the way I plan them, it'll be my *big* secret.

"Reading" Your Seller

Who the seller is and what he or she does will influence your offer. For example, an elderly widow who inherited the property might not be as familiar with market values as a middle-aged lawyer notorious as a land speculator.

If you're buying a lot in a relatively new subdivision, the seller may not be willing to negotiate at all. For the first year or so, developers are usually flush with optimism and very conscious of their development costs. Even more important, the developer realizes that pricing decisions made on early lot sales affect the price structure of the remaining lots. You may, however, be able to extract a little something extra out of him, such as an up-to-date perc test or a survey. In any case, be sure the project is feasible at the price you must pay the developer.

Trust Your Feasibility Analysis

Write the seller's asking price or the seller's best counteroffer in your feasibility analysis. What's the profit if you pay that price? Suppose there's no way you can pay the asking price and still make money on the deal. What then? Explaining the problem to your seller may not help at all. A seller who saw a miserable little lot down the street go for a big price probably won't be at all impressed by your data.

If the seller won't budge, you've got no choice. Go on to some other parcel. What everyone else is doing or what the seller thinks the property is worth is irrelevant. Believe what you conclude from your feasibility analysis. Don't lose your sanity just because others are losing theirs. A good feasibility analysis is the best defense I know against persuasive sellers and aggressive real estate agents. If a spec home won't work for you, *it doesn't matter what others are paying*.

Keep in mind that the invisible hand of the marketplace tends to inflate land prices until all profit you might be able to get out of the land itself is squeezed out. The market abhors a free lunch. That doesn't mean spec builders have to work for free. They don't. They just have to watch the numbers a little more closely and pass up the deals that can't pan out.

Making the Offer

I usually start at 25 percent below what I feel is the fair market value. A lower offer probably won't be considered by the seller. An offer at 25 percent less than market value is low enough to guarantee a profit (if the offer is accepted) while keeping the door ajar for subsequent negotiations.

Making the right offer the first time is the key to a successful negotiation, in my opinion. An offer too low won't elicit a reasonable counteroffer. The seller will assume you're not serious. Most sellers only want to deal with quality buyers. Remember, you're negotiating more than just price, you also need time.

Details in Your Offer

Now that you've selected a site, your primary concerns become price, title and time.

- ■ Price. Obviously, you need a price that makes the project feasible.

- ■ Title. The title is either clear or it isn't. You want to see a clear chain of title ending with the current seller. The title company is your best source of information on title to the property.

- ■ Time. The sale has to close on your schedule, not when the seller needs the cash. Don't consign yourself to the tender mercies of an indifferent fate. Specify very clearly what has to happen before the sale closes.

Time Before Closing

You need time to determine if the project is feasible. You don't want to spend the time and money planning a spec home if the property may be sold to someone else before planning is complete. But buying property before you do the essential planning is even worse. The best solution is to build adequate time into the purchasing process. That's usually called *tying up the land*.

You need the seller's consent to tie up the land. You get that consent by convincing the seller that you're both serious and prudent.

Earlier, I explained the disadvantage of making ridiculous offers. Serious buyers don't come in with lowball prices. It's important that you appear to be serious in the seller's eyes. As a serious, prudent buyer, you need time to decide. Explain to your seller that anything can go wrong during the development process. You need time to check out potential problems. There's no other way to be sure the project will fly. Closing on land you can't use would be folly. A reasonable seller will understand this.

You want to know as much about the property as you can before making the offer. That's why you completed the preliminary steps in the development schedule before doing so. It's much easier to get the price adjusted during the negotiations than it is to negotiate an adjustment after the contract is signed.

There are two ways to gain enough time. One is by taking an option on the land. The other is by negotiating a contingency contract. An option gives you the exclusive right to buy the land at a specified price until a certain date. A contingency contract gives you the right to back out of the deal if certain contingencies aren't met.

The Contingency Agreement

My advice is to avoid any mention of options. When people think about options, they assume option money will be paid. That kind of money isn't refundable. It's compensation to the seller for taking the property off the market. As a buyer, I never want to pay for something I may not use. Fortunately, there's a much better choice: A standard purchase contract with contingencies built in. The net effect is the same. I have the right to back out if the deal won't fly. The difference is that there's no option price in a contingency contract. It's like an option to buy, but the option comes free.

Your challenge in drafting a contingency contract is to:

1) Frame contingencies so they achieve the desired result.

2) Convince the seller to accept those contingencies.

I use a contingency agreement addendum like that shown in Figure 5-2. I've used this as an addendum to my purchase agreements for many years. It's saved me from mistakes many times and has never cost me more than a little ink.

Most landowners have at some time made an offer to purchase property. That offer was probably contingent on financing. So the seller is no doubt familiar with the notion of a contingency contract, an agreement that becomes binding on the buyer only if certain events happen. You'll note, however, that Figure 5-2 never mentions financing. This is a psychological edge. You'll give the impression that financing is no problem and that you're a very able buyer. It may or may not be a problem. Either way, it's your business, not the seller's. The contingency here, as far as the seller is concerned, and hopefully as far as you're concerned too, isn't financing. Instead, it's all the other details you have to work out.

The clause in Figure 5-2, "at a cost satisfactory to Buyer," gives you broad discretion. It can mean almost anything you want it to mean. If the cost isn't satisfactory (in your opinion), you can walk away from the deal and get your deposit back.

Preserving the right to back out as long as possible reduces your risk. That's important. As time passes, the deal may begin to look either more or less attractive. If it becomes a better deal, you want the seller obligated. If it begins to go sour, you may want to walk.

I've never had a seller force me into buying land I couldn't use. But you may. After all, "A deal is a deal. I understand your situation and I'd really like to let you out of the contract, but my sick mother needs an operation and I don't have any choice." Anything can happen — or as Murphy's Law puts it "Anything that can go wrong, will."

I'm not suggesting that you tie up a seller's land frivolously. But you've got a lot more to lose than the seller does.

Contingency Agreement

On this _____ day of _____

_____ (Buyer) agrees to buy and

_____ (Seller) agrees to sell property known as

_____

in the county of _____ for a price of $_____.

This contract is contingent upon the Buyer obtaining building permits, licenses and approvals from governmental authorities and at a cost satisfactory to Buyer to build a

_____

on the property. Buyer has _____ days, or as soon as possible from the date of this agreement to satisfy this contingency.

If, for any reason, buyer cannot obtain approvals required by government to construct the building intended at a cost satisfactory to Buyer, Buyer may, at his option, elect not to purchase the property and all earnest money and deposits made by the Buyer to Seller will be refunded. If Buyer elects not to purchase the property, all surveys, plans and engineering reports relating to the property which have been purchased by Buyer will be given to Seller at no cost to Seller.

Seller grants Buyer and his agents the right to enter onto the property for the purpose of conducting engineering studies and tests needed to qualify for building permits or government approvals. Seller agrees to extend this contract for a reasonable length of time to satisfy governmental authorities. Seller agrees to execute any documents reasonably necessary to obtain the permits, licenses and approvals required by governmental authorities before construction can begin. Seller warrants that there are no leases encumbering the property at the time of execution of this agreement except as identified below:

_____

At the end of _____ days from this date, Buyer shall have the right to extend this contract for _____ successive 30-day periods by delivering to Seller on or before the fifth day of each 30-day period a nonrefundable $500 payment. Buyer has the right to purchase the property at any time during these 30-day extension periods. These payments, when made, will be credited against the purchase price of the property at closing. In the event the property is not purchased during an extension period, these payments will be forfeited but all other earnest money will be refunded to Buyer.

_____   _____
Buyer   Seller

_____   _____
Buyer   Seller

Figure 5-2 The contingency agreement

Selling the Contingency Agreement

Before presenting the offer and the contingency agreement, I recommend that you enlighten the seller a little. The seller must know that you're willing to pay a reasonable price (in your opinion), but you can't buy land you can't use.

Tactfully make the seller aware of the obstacles you face and the risks you'll have to take to build on this property. A seller who understands the challenge tends to become a partner in a common cause. Make the seller understand that both buyer and seller have a mutual interest in the successful development of the land.

If project costs escalate for reasons that aren't anticipated, you won't ask the seller to lower his selling price. All you're asking for is a contingency contract, like the one in Figure 5-2. If the seller balks, use the argument that any other builder he may sell to will run into the same roadblock, should there be one, and need the same protection.

If the seller won't buy this argument, don't burn any bridges. Pleasantly offer to make yourself available in the future to discuss the matter.

Here's an excellent way to persuade the seller to accept your contingency contract. Make an unsolicited offer to turn over all surveys, site plans, perc tests and reports if the deal doesn't go through. This does three things:

- It alerts the seller that you're willing and able to spend money on the parcel.

- It enhances your image as a serious buyer.

- It gives something of value to the seller if the deal doesn't go through.

Offering something for free may help you negotiate a better deal later on more important issues such as the price and time. Notice that this concession costs you very little. If the deal doesn't materialize, the surveys, site plans, perc tests and reports are of no value to you anyway.

Getting Even More Time

You not only need time, you need enough of it. There's much that needs to be done before closing on the land. Many delays will be beyond your control. For this reason you need the right to extend the contract. By the end of the initial contract period, you'll have spent quite a bit of time and money. So you don't want pressure to close on the land before your research is completed.

You not only need time, you need enough of it.

You intend to move right along with the work, of course, but you don't want to be rushed. That's why there's provision for extensions in the contingency agreement. These extensions, however, you're willing to pay for. This reassures the seller, since time is his enemy as well as yours. Most sellers get a little anxious if you propose to tie up the land beyond some point, even with the freebies you've offered.

If an extension of time is required, you'll have a reasonably clear idea that the project is feasible. You should be willing to risk some money. Be sure that extension amounts are reasonable and will be applied to the purchase price. Your offer to pay for extensions after some period of time should make the seller more willing to accept your contingency contract.

Give-and-Take Negotiations

I recommend being generous on the little items and very tight-fisted on the land price. First, offer to split the title company fees and survey cost. If the seller isn't willing to split these costs, offer to pay for them yourself. It's surprising how some sellers can be negotiated to shave thousands off the purchase price but insist on full price for insignificant trifles. Don't make that mistake yourself.

There are advantages to paying for the survey yourself.

■ First, you get the surveyor you want.

■ Second, you have control over what the survey shows. For example, the seller won't want to pay for a topographical survey. But for you, getting a topo map now may save money later. My advice is to have your surveyor shoot the grades during the initial survey.

■ Third, you have more control over time. The survey is likely the first thing you hire out. Finishing it quickly lets you move on to other issues faster.

I recommend working step by step during the development process. There is an inherent disadvantage in that you must finish A before you move on to B. That's slower, but you reduce your risk exposure significantly.

When You've Got a Deal

You can afford to work slowly and cautiously before the land purchase agreement is signed. In fact, it's wise to take your time and consider all the alternatives. The less money you have invested, the less pressure there is to do something. Once you've signed an agreement, however, delays become much more costly. The contingency contract is a lot like the time delay on a building's alarm system. You've turned on the system but you've got time to leave. Use this time to your advantage finishing the development process and tying up any loose ends. If you discover some dreadful flaw in your data at the last moment, you still have time and a way to back out. Yes, there will probably be some financial loss. But better a small loss now than a big one later. Remember too that everything doesn't ride on one horse. There's always another piece of buildable land.

Chapter 6
Working With the Designer

In the area of design, I believe the builder needs to be a generalist. Don't even think about designing the house yourself. You don't have the skills and your time is too valuable. Frankly, I don't really know much about design. I know that you need bedrooms, bathrooms, a kitchen, living room, and some way to get into the house. That's about it. The market tells me all I need to know and my designer keeps me out of trouble with the plans. That's his (or her) job.

Find a designer you trust, make your wishes clear, and delegate the responsibility. Make sure he or she has a wide variety of stock plans to choose from. By now you know what's selling in the marketplace, so you can pick a stock plan that fits the bill. If the plan doesn't have a deck and your market wants one, you add a deck to the stock plan. No big deal. That's what I call innovative design. If it gets more complicated than that, you need to find a designer with a larger file of stock plans.

What's good design? Good design is what sells. Period. That's all the builder needs to know. So here's the real question: What design elements will attract or repel prospective buyers? These are important decisions that are bound to affect the success or failure of your project. Obviously, this is one more opportunity to use what you've learned about buyer preferences in your community.

Balance Aesthetics, Function and Cost

Unfortunately, you can't consider design by itself. Every design decision has an effect on cost. The design has to be right, of course. But the asking price also has to be right — both for the product you're offering and for the prospective home buyers.

First, make sure that the design doesn't lead to excessive construction costs. But don't go overboard with efficiency. Let's say you find a clever way to reduce bathroom construction costs by $100. Will you lose ten times that amount when the house sits unsold because you tried to cut corners? Within reason, I'd rather waste money in the bathroom than worry about it. Sometimes it's good business to be a little inefficient and give the buyers a little more for their money. The cost will be minimal, and you'll gain a satisfied customer who thinks he's getting just a little bit more than he paid for.

Every design decision requires weighing aesthetics and function against cost. Good design for a spec home means balancing the cost of each feature against the value prospective buyers are likely to perceive in that feature. We're dealing here with style and vogue, likes and dislikes. The considerations are subtle and the variables are infinite. I suppose that's why some spec builders thrive and prosper while others get stuck with inventory that won't sell. Building the right house for the right market and at the right price is never easy. *So use your market study. It's your best guide.*

It isn't easy to keep a tight rein on costs. While the design possibilities are unlimited, you have to set limits. There's no use considering more than a small number of the most appealing alternatives. Your buyers (or their lenders) won't pay for most of what a designer could do with unlimited funds. You have to be very practical when making design decisions. *Always go with what the market will pay for.*

Your job, as a builder, is to construct the most aesthetically pleasing and functional homes possible within the budget of prospective buyers. Work with your designer to avoid spending money on anything that won't increase buyer appeal. Trust your designer to understand the rules of efficient layout, traffic patterns and practicality, just like your plumber knows how to route water lines. If the designer doesn't do the kind of work you expect, find one who does.

It Comes Down to Value

Naturally, you want to offer prospective buyers the most house possible for the dollar. Home buyers are shopping for enclosed space. The more, the better. Most won't think to ask about the cost of the home per square foot of floor (or per cubic foot under the roof). But nearly all will instinctively recognize good value.

Look for opportunities to deliver real value at modest cost. Try to improve on your competition. If you have a good idea, try it. If it saves money and yields good results, do more of the same. Don't ignore even minor savings. Small improvements repeated many times can make a major difference. But don't be too cheap. In some areas, the cost of fluted columns is a good investment, even though they have no function except to make the house more attractive to buyers.

Basic Design Decisions

I'm going to offer some general observations and guidelines you can follow when designing a spec home. Of course, I can't recommend one style over another. I'll leave the specifics to you and your designer. But there are some generalizations that every spec builder has to understand. For example, I recommend following, not innovating, on design issues. Every community has examples of what works

Z-frame houses: summer cottage ideas that failed.

and what doesn't. The ultimate measure of good taste in home design is what sells the best in your community. Supplement that information with the advice of design professionals who deal with problems like these every day.

Don't overbuild or underbuild. Of course, you want to offer better value than other builders are promoting. But the market prefers well-established norms. Good design is more concerned with what the market wants than with charm or novelty in home design.

The Layout

The interior layout of the house must be appropriate for the size and price range of your spec home. For example, in my area most builders offer three-bedroom homes with a combination living room/family room rather than a separate living room. Can you afford to offer a separate living room in your design? Or will it cost more than it brings in? If most spec builders in your community offer a separate living room and family room only in four-bedroom homes, that's probably what you should do. I recommend following the lead set by others.

The Exterior

The exterior of your spec home should fit in with adjacent property. Drive through the neighborhood looking at roof lines, overhangs and window openings. Stay away from unusual or "advanced" designs. While unusual design may attract coverage in your local newspaper, it may also scare away prospective buyers.

Avoid including too many of your personal preferences in architectural aesthetics. Most prospective buyers simply want a comfortable home. They aren't trying to make a personal design statement. Your buyers probably don't want a truly unique home — or the attention that goes with an outlandish design.

Suppose you find the one-in-a-million prospective buyer who loves your choice of high-tech Bauhaus styling. What then? Is that prospective buyer going to commit? Not likely! He (or she) probably understands that a house is an investment as well as a home. They'll want to sell it eventually. When that time comes, will there be many buyers who appreciate high-tech Bauhaus? The market will probably exhibit the same reservations then as it does today.

If you stray too far from the beaten path, you're left with an uncomfortably small segment of the market. Conform, don't innovate! That's your best guarantee of making a positive contribution to the local housing stock and healthy deposits at your bank.

Interior Design

Some spec builders do their own interior design — but I recommend using an interior design coordinator. For a small fee you'll get assistance in selecting exterior and interior paint colors, carpet, fireplace design, molding, and other finishing touches. You can have input if you want to, but getting a second opinion is easily worth the fee. Try to find an interior designer who works with other builders. You're looking for someone with a knack for colors, insight about what the market wants, and the ability to work with buyers if the home is sold before completion. An experienced interior designer can recommend sources for materials and provide names of contractors with a reputation for doing good interior finish work.

Set Design Limits

Never cut corners on something that will reduce the structural integrity of the building. Don't allow yourself, your designer, your subcontractors or material suppliers to do anything to cause a safety hazard or promote premature deterioration or structural failure. The building code sets practical limits on shortcuts and innovative design. You can't do what the code doesn't allow. The code (and building inspectors) tend to control quality on the job. Many spec home builders use the building code as a lever to insure that subcontractors do their work properly. My advice is to always use the code to your own advantage, not to have it used against you. Design the home so you avoid anything the inspector may consider controversial. There's no profit in an argument with the inspector, but there can be a significant loss.

Here are some functional design issues you need to check on in the working drawings:

- Are chases in the framing properly designed for plumbing stacks?

- Do door swings disrupt traffic patterns or block access to cabinets?

- Is space available under bathrooms for plumbing drains?

- Do stairwells leave adequate head clearance and enough turning space at the stairway top and bottom?

- If the fireplace chimney is on the exterior, be sure it doesn't encroach on setback lines.

- The kitchen is a focal point for potential buyers. Space offered here creates sales interest.

- Attic space is cheap. Find a way to make the attic useful for storage. It just takes planning and a few pieces of plywood. If feasible, build stairs rather than using a pull-down stair system to the attic.

- Put in full basements when possible. A basement adds a lot of space at little additional cost.

- Keep traffic off the root system of trees during construction. Trees are assets until they die. Then they need to be removed, which is expensive.

■ Wood decks add perceived floor area at modest cost. Using decks outside windows and doors tends to blend interior and exterior areas together.

■ Avoid retaining walls whenever possible. They're expensive, can be a source of problems later, and rarely add value equivalent to their cost.

Keep the Plans Simple

Complicated plans can be a handicap.

Complicated plans can be a handicap. A single-family spec house is a relatively uncomplicated project. I recommend keeping the plans as simple as possible. The designer should include just enough detail to get the job done. The minimum required to get a building permit should be plenty. Your subcontractors and material suppliers are familiar with standard construction practice. If you've avoided unusual or nonstandard construction, as I suggest, the plans don't have to be detailed and complex. Simple plans tend to simplify bidding and reduce both the construction and design costs.

The Specifications

Your designer will have a standard set of specs. Most of the information in these specs will be technical, self-evident and unbearably dull reading for both you and your subcontractors. Your framer knows how to frame a house and doesn't want any more direction than absolutely necessary. If there's a technical question, the framer would probably prefer to check with the inspector or building department.

I recommend providing your own specs to cover design elements that are either nonstandard or require a closer reading of the plans. There's more information on this subject in Chapter 9.

One word of caution about plans and specs. Don't wait too long. Leave enough time for inspiration and refining your design decisions on paper. It's a waste of your time and money to release incomplete or incorrect plans to your bidders. When the plans go out for bid, you'll have plenty of work to do, and you don't need a lot of objections from the subcontractors and material suppliers reviewing the plans.

Here are my last words on design: Get satisfaction from your profit margin, not your design innovations. You're trying to make a living in a very competitive business, not building a museum. If prospective buyers won't pay for exceptional design, there's no sense in offering it. Most importantly, *go with the market.* Build what will sell. That's good design.

Chapter 7
Lining Up the Financing

Most builders get into trouble because of financing.

That's like saying people get into trouble because they're born. There's no way to avoid the inevitable. Spec home building and financing troubles are inseparable for all but the lucky few who can build without borrowing. For the rest of us, interest payments begin with the first draw and continue relentlessly, twenty-four hours a day, seven days a week, until the project is sold.

You'll avoid trouble *most of the time* if you have a big enough loan and the right kind of financing. That's what this chapter is about. You'll avoid trouble nearly *all the time* if you build within the feasibility analysis budget and sell the house as predicted in your market study.

The Loan Amount

The market value or construction cost establishes the upper limit of what you can borrow. Your banker will want to lend a percentage of one or the other. That percentage is called the *loan-to-value ratio* or *loan-to-cost ratio*, and it's usually between 70 and 75 percent. Naturally, this ratio depends on market conditions, the bank's willingness to lend, the perceived risk and your desirability as a borrower. I've even gotten 80 percent loans, but I'm afraid those are a thing of the past. You'll prefer your lender to use the market value ratio, especially if you're trying to finance 100 percent of your construction costs. Unfortunately, your lender may insist on the *loan-to-cost* formula instead because it reduces their risk. Today's construction loan terms and amounts are tied to conditions that vary month-to-month. So much depends on the climate in the building industry, interest rates, and how desperate your lender is to get more loans in their portfolio. If you own the land free and clear, the construction loan should cover construction costs. Your lender may want a lower ratio to minimize risk of loss if market values fall. The lender's loan committee won't have much latitude in setting the loan-to-value or loan-to-cost ratio. That's a result of policy decisions by the lender as dictated by government regulations.

"I'm sorry, the possibility that you may have won $10 million in the Publisher's Clearing House sweepstakes won't do as collateral."

Naturally, your lender would like to see you putting plenty of your own cash into the project. There's likely to be some difference of opinion on that point. Lenders are more interested in security than in the additional interest they might make on a larger loan. What your lender would like to see you put in as cold, hard cash and what you're willing or able to invest may not be the same figure. Even if you do have the money, you may prefer to keep it for yourself. Remember, though, that the less you borrow, the less total interest you pay.

Financing the Project

Your feasibility study, described in Chapter 3, not only provides you with an estimate of the project's profit potential but also an estimate of costs. That makes it easy to determine the amount you need to borrow. All you do is add up the cost columns. For example, suppose your feasibility study shows that the project costs are as follows:

Land	$22,500
Development costs	$7,600
Financing costs	$5,250
Construction costs	$79,500
Total costs	$115,075

Assume that your market study shows that the market value of the finished home is $150,000.

If your lender is willing to make you a loan for 70 percent of the market value, that's a loan for a total of $105,000 (150,000 x 0.70 = 105,000). You'll need to kick in the difference between the total cost ($115,075) and the loan amount ($105,000). That comes to a total of $10,075 from other sources or your own money.

But if you can get a loan-to-value ratio of 75 percent, then the whole picture changes. At the 75 percent ratio the total amount of your loan is $112,500 (150,000 x 0.75 = 112,500). That's less than $3,000 short of your estimated (and perhaps slightly conservative) total costs. If you can negotiate your way into this higher loan-to-value ratio you may be able to virtually "finance out" your whole project. In good times, this can and does happen. In bad times, when banks are running scared, don't count on it.

Of course, each project is different. Your financing depends on many factors, including current costs, the projected sales price, and your relationship with your lender. It also depends on how efficient you are at purchasing the land, arranging your financing, holding down construction costs, accurately predicting the market, and any number of other skills. Because there are so many variables, there are no hard and fast rules you can depend on. Unless you own the land free and clear, there's usually a very close margin between having to put a good chunk of your own money into the project and letting the bank carry more of the load. However, if you're skilled enough *and* gain the confidence of your lender, you can eliminate a good part of that margin. Putting it all together right is what makes one spec builder consistently more successful than another.

Until you prove yourself, your lender will be very conservative in determining what loan-to-value or loan-to-cost ratio to offer you. Spec builders want to take risks; lenders don't. If the project should go into foreclosure, your lender will want to recover as much of the loan principal as possible, even if the property must be sold at auction.

However, don't be frightened into borrowing too little money. The loan should provide enough cash to finish the house and hold it for a period of time until it sells. If costs are lower than expected, or if the home sells sooner than expected, you may not have to draw down the full loan amount. Interest accrues only on the amount borrowed, not what's left in the kitty, so you'll be ahead in the game. As a spec builder, you're paid to take risks. Those who survive in this business learn to contain those risks.

Finding the Right Lender

Broaden your search to include the larger commercial banks.

Start by talking to a loan officer at your own bank. Then, if necessary, broaden your search to include the larger commercial banks and thrift associations active in your community. Ask if they're currently making construction loans. If so, what interest rates and costs could you expect? What are the loan requirements? The more lenders you talk to, the better. Loan officers will have a wealth of valuable information about the spec building market in your community.

All lenders don't follow the same rules. You'll discover the lenders in your community have different loan requirements, loan costs, loan terms and interest rates. Shop around. Get the best deal you can. Narrow the field to those offering the most attractive terms.

While collecting this information, remember two things:

1) Lenders must make loans to stay in business.

2) Under that natty Brooks Brothers suit the loan officer is wearing is a stickler for details and specific performance on loan agreements. Loan officers tend to be good negotiators, but don't be afraid to press for the best deal you can get, both in mortgage terms and loan cost. Until loan documents are signed, you're still in the driver's seat, so negotiate for all it's worth.

Introduce Your Project

When you've found a loan officer willing to deal, discuss your plans for the project. Remember that both you and the lender are looking for a long-term relationship that's beneficial to both parties. As long as your ambitions fall within the lender's capacity, and as long as loan payoffs clip along at a satisfactory pace, you'll probably continue to use the same lender. Establishing a satisfactory relationship with one lender will reduce the time you spend searching for financing and filling out applications. It's a real comfort to know that financing will be ready when you're ready to jump.

Most spec home builders deal with only one lender. They change lenders reluctantly, usually because something went wrong with their usual source. Timely loan payoff (as forecast in your market study) is your best guarantee of a happy and extended relationship.

The Loan Request Package

When you've found a lender that's interested, begin by delivering a loan request package. This is your prospective lender's official introduction to the project. Figure 7-1A through J is sample loan request package. This package includes:

- Loan request letter

- Property description

- Location map

- Survey

- Project characteristics

- Site plan

- Biographical sketch of builder

- Financial statement

- Elevation plan

- Floor plan

The package should provide the lender with just enough information to evaluate the project. In the biographical sketch, stick to the facts. Omit the sales pitch. Your lender has heard too much puffery from loan applicants already.

The purpose of the loan request package is to provide a concise overview of your project. The package should include all the essential information needed to make a preliminary evaluation of the project. Most of this package will be presented to the lender's loan committee when that committee is ready to approve the loan. Of course, you can't anticipate everything the loan committee may need. But the package is a good place to start. The loan officer will ask for additional information as it's needed.

HOME BUILDER'S CONSTRUCTION COMPANY
621 Randolph Road
Newport News, VA   23605

9 July 1994

Dear Sir or Madam,

The accompanying information describes a construction loan request for a new single family house to be built at 1732 Valley View Lane, Newport News, VA.

The house will have three bedrooms and two baths with full basement. The total net heated floor area will be 1,547 square feet. Construction will be brick veneer and masonite siding.

Home Builder's Construction Company will act as General Contractor. The sale will be handled by Happy Homes Realty.

I am requesting a 75 percent loan-to-value ratio.

I hope you will find this loan attractive. If I can be of further assistance please let me know.

Sincerely,

Ed Kopp

Ed Kopp
President

Figure 7-1A Loan request letter

LOCATION:
1732 Valley View Lane in the New Hope Subdivision, Newport News, Virginia.

SIZE:
The property dimensions are: 125 feet by 175 feet, or 21,875 square feet, with 125 feet of frontage on Valley View Lane.

UTILITIES:
All utilities are available to the property. Utilities are provided by: Tidewater Gas and Electric, Bell Atlantic, Hampton Roads Cable TV and the Newport News Water Works Board. Sewer is available to the site.

TOPOGRAPHY:
The site slopes from left to right.

ZONING:
Zoning is R-1 (Single Family)

SUPPORT FACILITIES:
The site is within 10 minutes driving time of the Southgate Mall in Mountain Park, a bedroom community of Newport News, and 20 minutes from downtown Norfolk, VA. Schools, restaurants, libraries, grocery stores, parks, banks, and such are all within easy driving distance of the site.

LEGAL:
Lot 72, Block 12, New Hope Subdivision

Figure 7-1B Property description

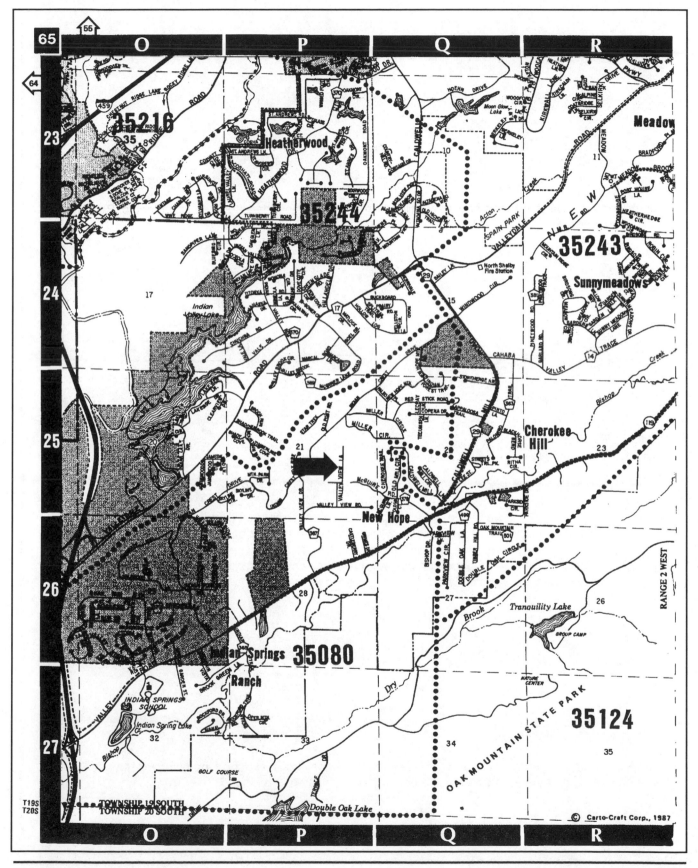

Figure 7-1C   Location map

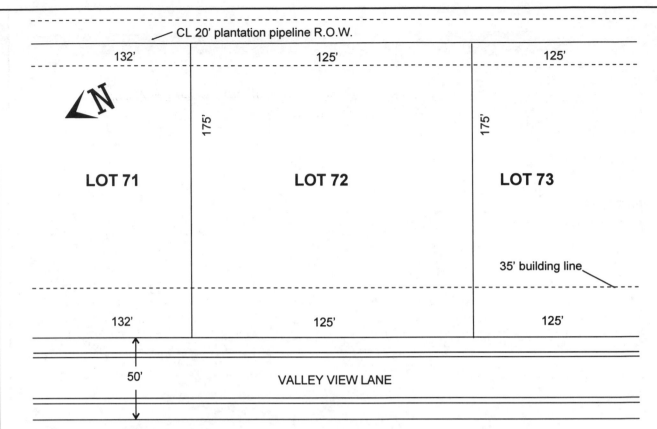

STATE OF VIRGINIA
JEFFERSON COUNTY

I, T. R. Smith a Registered Surveyor, do hereby certify that this is a true and correct plat or map of Lot __72__ Block __12__ of New Hope Subdivision as recorded in Map Book __129__ Page __82__ in the Probate Office Jefferson County, Virginia, and that there are no visible encroachments of buildings, rights of way, easements or joint driveways over or across said land except as shown; there are no visible encroachments by electrical or telephone wire (excluding wires which serve the premises only) or structures or supports therefor, including poles, anchors and guy wires, on or over said premises except as shown.

According to my survey this __13th__ day of __May, 1994__.

T. R. Smith
T. R. Smith. Reg. No. 56789

This is to certify that I have consulted the Federal Insurance Administration Flood Hazard Boundary Map and found that the above described property is not located in a Flood Prone Area.

Figure 7-1D Survey

CONSTRUCTION:
This single family house will be three bedrooms and two baths with brick veneer and Masonite siding, full basement and gas heat. The back door will lead to an outside deck. It should be completed by August, 1994.

NET HEATED AREA:
1,547 square feet

PARKING:
Two parking spaces will be provided in the basement.

MARKETING CHARACTERISTICS:
The location of this project is excellent. With good schools and easy access to the Interstate, the Mountain Park Community has traditionally been an attractive and popular mid-priced bedroom community for homeowners working in the Greater Norfolk Metropolitan Area. The New Hope Subdivision in the Mountain Park Community has done very well since the beginning of its development in 1991. All houses have sold either before or within a reasonable period of time following completion of construction.

PROJECTED SALES PRICE:
$150,000

Figure 7-1E   Project characteristics

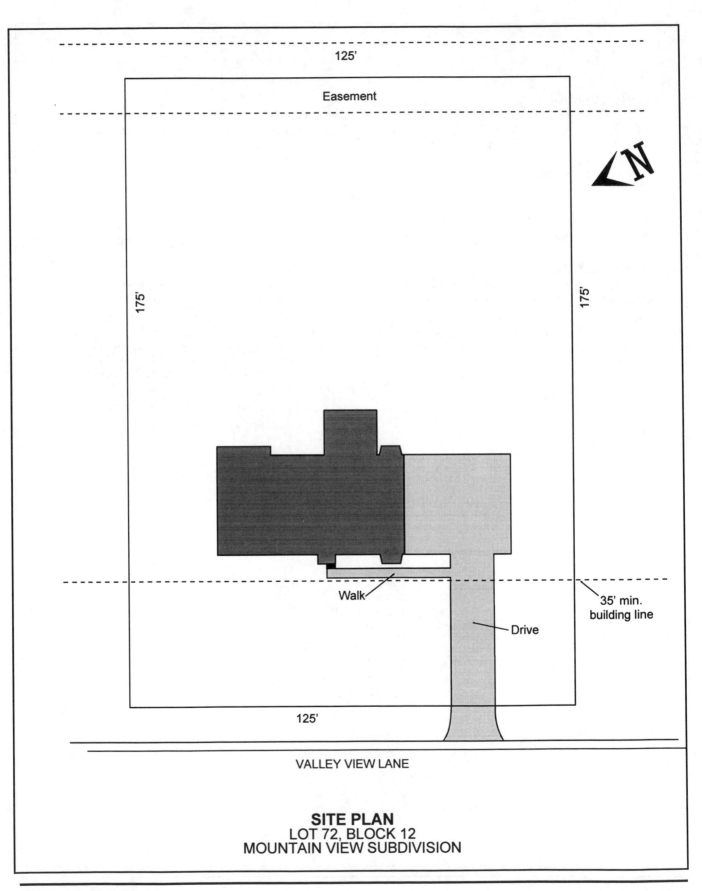

SITE PLAN
LOT 72, BLOCK 12
MOUNTAIN VIEW SUBDIVISION

Figure 7-1F   Site plan

The builder is: Ed Kopp.

Mr. Kopp is 38 years of age. He is a native of Newport News and holds a Master's Degree in History from Old Dominion University.

Mr. Kopp has been active in the construction business for more than 15 years. During the past few years he has focused on building single-family speculative housing. His success in this field has been considerable. During the past two years alone he has built and sold three such homes.

Mr. Kopp is the owner and president of Home Builder's Construction Company.

Mr. Kopp will act as General Contractor for the project.

Figure 7-1G Biographical sketch of builder

/AmSouth

Confidential Financial Statement

Name _____   Business/Employer Name _____

Address _____   Position or Occupation _____

City _____ State _____ Zip _____   Phone: Business _____ Home _____

Social Security Number _____   Social Security Number (spouse, if joint) _____

For the purpose of obtaining credit from you from time to time, I submit the following statement of my financial condition

as of _____ , 19 _____ .

ASSETS SOLELY OWNED
(List only those assets to which you have sole legal title)

Cash On Hand & In This Bank	$
Cash: Other Banks—See Schedule A	
U.S. Government & Marketable Securities—See Schedule B	
Non-Marketable Securities—Schedule B	
Real Estate—See Schedule C	
Notes and Accounts Receivable	
Automobiles	
Other Personal Property	
Cash Value Life Insurance—Schedule D	
Other Assets:	
TOTAL ASSETS (Sole)	

LIABILITIES AND NET WORTH
(List all liabilities, joint or otherwise)

Notes Payable to Banks—Schedule E	$
Notes Payable to Others—Schedule E	
Real Estate Mortgages Payable—See Schedule C	
Accounts Payable	
Unpaid Income Taxes: Fed ☐ State ☐	
Loans on Life Insurance Policies	
Other Liabilities:	
TOTAL LIABILITIES	$
(total liabilities)	
NET WORTH	$
& NET WORTH	$

ASSETS JOINT
(List all assets)

Cash On Hand & In This Bank	
Cash: Other Banks—See Sched.	
U.S. Government & Marketable S Schedule B	
Non-Marketable Securities—Schedule B	
Real Estate—See Schedule C	
Notes and Accounts Receivable	
Automobiles	
Other Personal Property	
Cash Value Life Insurance—Schedule D	
Other Assets:	
TOTAL ASSETS (Joint)	$

SOURCES OF INCOME
For the year ended _____

Salary	$
Bonuses and Commissions	
Dividends	
Rental Income (net of expenses & debt service)	
Other Income:	
Alimony, child support or separate maintenance income need not be revealed if you do not wish to have it considered as a basis for obtaining credit.	
TOTAL INCOME	$

MONTHLY EXPENDITURES

Mortgage/Rent	$
Insurance	$
Car Payments	$
Installment Notes	$
Alimony	$

CONTINGENT LIABILITIES

As endorser, co-maker or guarantor	$
On leases or contracts	$
Legal claims	$
Contested income tax liens	$
Other special debts:	$

GENERAL INFORMATION

Are any assets pledged? See Schedules.	
Have you executed a will?	
If so, name of Executor:	
Are you a partner in any firm?	
Are you defendant in any suits or legal actions?	
Have you ever taken bankruptcy?	

Form 100011
bkF1 (6/88)

Figure 7-1H Financial statement (Builder should request financial statement form acceptable to lender.)

If the space provided below is not sufficient, additional schedules may be attached.

Schedule A—CASH IN BANKS

Name of Bank	Type of Account	Type of Ownership	On Deposit
			$
			$
			$
			$

Schedule B—SECURITIES OWNED

Face Value—Bonds Shares—Stock	Description	Type of Ownership	Cost	Market Value	Amount Pledged to Secure Loans
			$	$	$

Schedule C—REAL ESTATE OWNED

Description of Property and Improvements	Date Acquired	Cost	Market Value	Mortgage Payable			
				Balance Due	Payment	Maturity	To Whom Payable
		$	$	$	$		

Schedule D—LIFE INSURANCE

Company			Other Loans— Policy as Collateral	Beneficiary
		$	$	

SAMPLE

Schedule E—NOTES PAYABLE

Name of Bank/Others	Type of Loan	Maturity Date	Amount of Loan	Monthly Payment	Collateral (If Any)
			$	$	

The foregoing has been carefully read by me and is given to you for the purpose of obtaining credit from time to time in whatever form. I hereby certify it is a true and correct exhibit of my financial condition and may be treated by you as a continuing statement thereof until replaced by a new statement or until I specifically notify you of change therein. In consideration of such credit which you may advance me. I agree that if at any time this statement shall prove incorrect, in your judgement, as a statement of my then condition, or if at any time by reason of insolvency, application for receiver, or any act or omission on my part in your judgement such credit is prejudiced or impaired, all or any of my obligations to you, whether direct, indirect, contingent or fixed shall immediately stand due and payable without demand upon or notice to me, and any money or other property owned by me and in your possession in whatever capacity may in your discretion be held and, without prior notice to me, sold and/or applied by you against any of my such obligations to you. You are authorized to check my credit and employment history and to answer questions about your credit experience with me.

Witness my hand and seal this _____ day of _____ , 19 _____ .

_____ (SEAL)

WITNESS:

_____ (SEAL)

_____

_____

Form 100011
bkF1 (6/88)

Figure 7-1H (cont.)   Financial statement (Builder should request financial statement form acceptable to lender.)

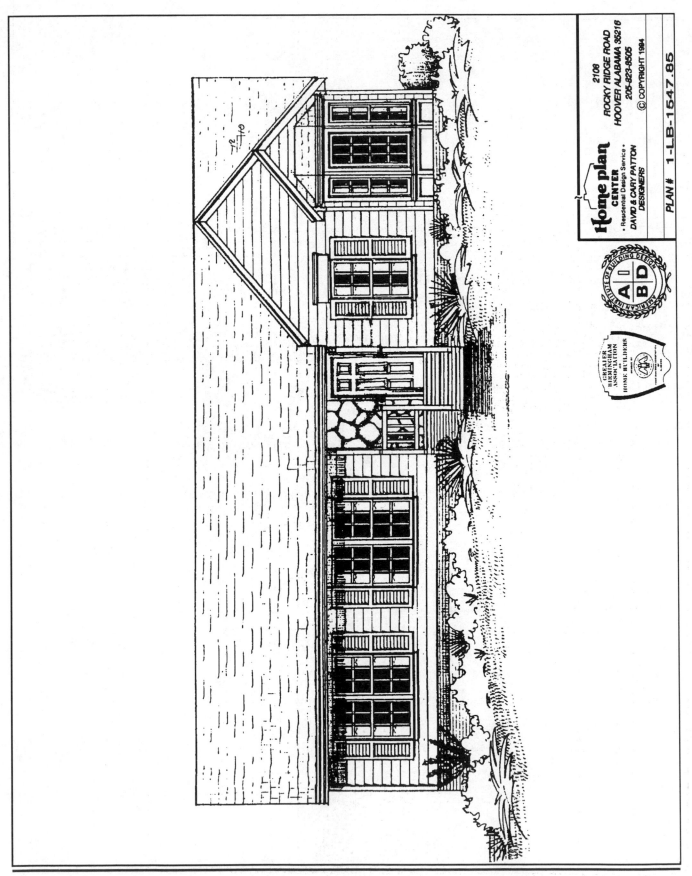

Figure 7-1I   Elevation plan

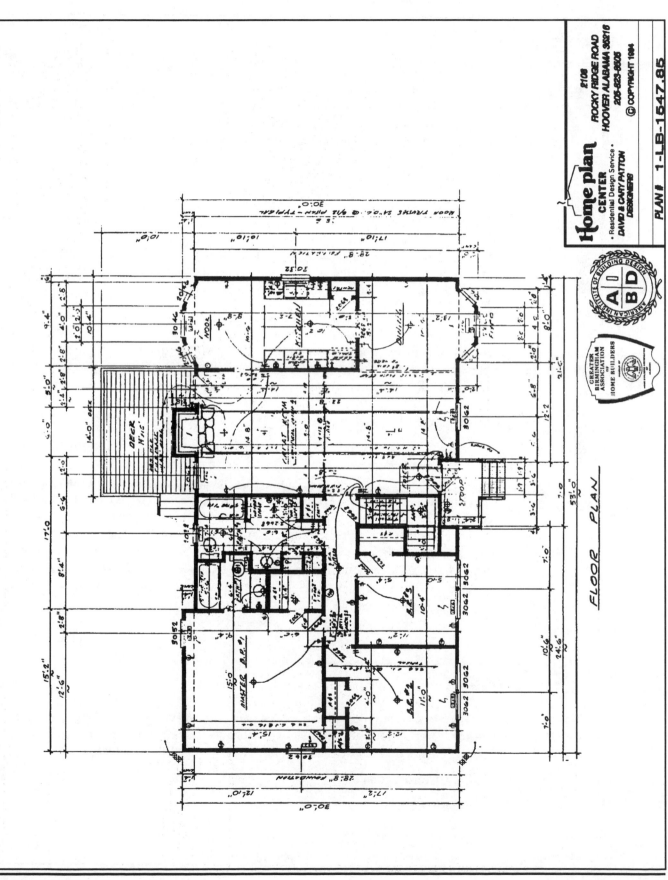

Figure 7-1J   Floor plan

Negotiating the Loan

If the loan request package appeals to your lender's appetite, you'll probably get a verbal offer (but not a commitment) on the loan. The offer will include a proposed interest rate, loan amount (based on some loan-to-value ratio), the term of the loan (try to get one year), and estimated loan fees and closing costs. If your loan officer doesn't mention the frequency and procedures for draws, be sure to ask about that now. You'll also need to know how they'll want you to make interest payments on the loan balance.

Getting a construction loan is a negotiating process. However, there are limits to what you can expect. You'll never get significantly more than other banks are offering. It's unlikely that you'll get everything you ask for. If you do, it's like a gift and lenders aren't charitable institutions. But they're also not looking for the opportunity to nail you to the wall. They just want to make a good, secure, profitable loan. If that's what you're asking for, you'll probably get it.

Your lender will use every legal means to improve loan security and profitability, in that order. Most loan officers are responsible for a portfolio of loans. Loan officers who make profitable loans that are repaid on time tend to get promoted. Loan officers who have too many loan defaults in their portfolios tend to have short careers. This doesn't mean you have to take a financial beating to win a lender's respect. It just means that you should use some discretion when deciding when to press an issue and when to back off.

Unless you're the biggest and most profitable spec builder in town, you'll probably have to compromise to get loans approved. Sometimes the lender won't negotiate. Then you'll have to give in. If the lender insists on a point, be quick to agree, but suggest making a tradeoff. Try to convert a loss into something graciously conceded. Help the loan officer understand that you're conceding this point but would appreciate something in return elsewhere. Be ready to concede the unattainable, then barter for concessions elsewhere. Whatever you do, don't beg — unless all else fails. *Then* get down on your knees. But keep in mind that no lender is going to make you an offer that varies much from what other lenders offer and what current loan policies permit.

Closing the Deal

Your lender will supply a written list of documents you'll have to provide before the loan can be approved. That list will probably include most of the documents in your original loan request package, plus some or all of the following:

1) Construction plans

2) Title Insurance Policy on the land

3) Draw request form

4) Letter confirming insurance coverage

5) Letter confirming lot zoning

6) Commitment letters from utility companies: electric, water, sewer and gas

7) Phase One Environmental Report

8) Revised cost breakdown

9) Copies of tax returns for three prior years

10) Building permit

11) Letter confirming that there are no outstanding assessments

12) Letter stating no asbestos will be used in construction

Your part in this process is to request the documents from the appropriate sources. The requirements of your lender and the community in which you will be working will determine just what documents you'll need to provide. There is no standard that works throughout the country. Just keep in mind that the lender's interest and yours coincide in making this project a success.

If you've done your homework (the market survey and the feasibility study) and if your personal financial situation is good, getting the loan approved is almost a sure thing. Convince the lender that your house can be sold at a good profit. Make it clear that you're financially sound and you're a good manager. Under those conditions, getting the loan approved should be one of the easier chores associated with the project.

Lending is a competitive business. If one lender turns you down, try another. They may be glad to oblige. If you can offer good collateral, a good loan size and rapid turnover, you're an ideal loan candidate.

Chapter 8
Cost Categories and Construction Forms

It's time to solicit bids for your project when:

■ Working drawings (plans) have been prepared

■ Specifications have been written

■ You've got a commitment for financing

■ You're satisfied that the land sale will close with no hitches

Estimating and bidding take time and effort. So it's wise to eliminate any uncertainty before passing out plans to prospective bidders.

Keeping Your Spec Home Project on Track

Construction of any building is a detailed, complex, expensive process requiring the cooperation of many individuals, contractors, subcontractors and government agencies. It's too expensive to do more than once and too permanent to do carelessly. Even worse, it's your money and your spec home that are at risk. If not managed correctly, you're either going to lose money or waste opportunities for major savings. Without careful supervision, a project too easily lapses into confusion. The wasted time and effort quickly become expensive for you and your subcontractors. There's also the additional risk of losing credibility with your lender and suppliers.

Fortunately, it doesn't take a genius to keep a construction project running smoothly. I recommend that you begin by breaking the project down into categories that are simpler to handle and understand. The way I do this is by using a set of three worksheets. We'll look at each of these in detail in this chapter. The forms help you watch the details in each cost category, and that helps keep the entire project on course.

The Cost Summary Worksheet

Use the worksheet in Figure 8-1 to collect onto one sheet the cost totals for every major construction cost category. When you add these cost totals to the project costs that we covered in the last chapter, the result is a complete cost list for your project.

The cost categories on the worksheet roughly follow the same sequence as the work itself. This is also the order in which you'll be receiving bills for work completed from your subs. In Chapter 10, "The Construction Schedule," we'll take a closer look at the right sequence of steps for construction to follow.

Obviously, the cost summary worksheet won't follow the construction order down to the last finishing nail. Some similar costs are grouped under broad cost categories, regardless of when the work will be done. These groupings make it easier to track and record costs in each category.

The Construction Cost Bidding Worksheet

This worksheet (Figure 8-2) is for you to collect bidding information. Use the top lines for notes and calculations, with a separate sheet for each cost category. The section at the bottom gives you room to record the best three bids by vendor, purchase order, number of units, price per unit and extended costs. That makes it easy to compare the bids and decide which one to choose.

The Construction Cost Breakdown

The construction cost breakdown (Figure 8-3) finishes up the chapter. I use this form to bid all the construction costs for a project. The form includes an item line for nearly every cost that's likely to come up when you're building a single-family spec home. There's also space for you to add your own extras. Begin by entering unit costs and quantities on each line that applies. Use the extension column to show the total for each row. The number of units multiplied by the cost per unit is the extended cost. The total of all the extended costs gives you a total construction cost.

I've used these forms as the basis for a spreadsheet, with all the item names listed and formulas embedded to calculate the extended cost. It's easy to print out a blank form to use for making notes and listing take-off calculations. Then I can enter the final information into the spreadsheet and have it calculate and total the extended costs.

You can also use this form as a checklist. Review this list; it may remind you of something you forgot or overlooked. No spec builder likes surprise costs. You can also use these basic cost categories to set up your bookkeeping system, probably using a computer spreadsheet or bookkeeping program.

You'll need to refer back to your notes and figures many times during construction. So it's smart to keep these forms in one convenient place. Get in the habit of making written notes about cost changes and completion milestones as they occur. Drop these notes into the project folder. It can save you hours of time looking for important information. The information you need most tends to be the information you threw away or misplaced. Construction work *is* detail work. Spec builders who are both organized and consistent tend to be consistently profitable.

Cost Summary Worksheet

Project Name: Date:

Code	Item	Estimated Costs	Actual Costs	Notes
00	**Construction Costs**			
01	Site Work			
04	Concrete			
07	Masonry			
10	Metal Work			
13	Rough Carpentry			
16	Exterior Door & Windows			
19	Plumbing			
22	Electrical			
25	HVAC			
28	Specialties			
31	Insulation			
34	Moisture Protection			
37	Drywall			
40	Cabinets and Countertops			
43	Finish Carpentry			
46	Hardware			
49	Painting and Wallpaper			
52	Exterior Flatwork & Paving			
55	Flooring			
58	Appliances			
61	Landscaping			
64	Furnishings & Equipment			
67	Salaries, Wages, Fees			
70	Equipment Costs			
73	Utility Costs			
76	Miscellaneous Job Costs			
	Total Construction Cost			

Item	Estimated Costs	Actual Costs	Notes
Project Costs			
Land Cost			
Development Costs			
Construction Costs			
Financing Costs			
Marketing and Closing Costs			
Total Project Cost			

Figure 8-1 Cost summary worksheet

Construction Cost Bidding Worksheet

Construction Cost Category:

Vendor	P.O. #	# Units	Price/Unit	Extended Cost
			Total	

Figure 8-2 Construction cost bidding worksheet

Construction Cost Breakdown

Project Name:_____ Date:_____ Page:_____

Code	Description	Quantity	Unit	Unit Price	Extended Cost
01	**Site Work**				
01000	Demolition contract		Lot		
01005	Sitework (before construction)		Lot		
01110	Grading layout		Lot		
01105	Tree removal		Lot		
01110	Loader		Hr		
01115	Trucks		Hr		
01120	Soil export/import		Lot		
01300	Sitework (after construction)		Lot		
01305	Loader		Hr		
01310	Trucks		Hr		
01315	Soil export/import		Lot		
01500	Off-site improvements		Lot		
01999	Total sales tax (if applicable)				
				Total Site Work	

Figure 8-3 Construction cost breakdown

Construction Cost Breakdown

Project Name:_____   Date:_____   Page:_____

Code	Description	Quantity	Unit	Unit Price	Extended Cost
04	**Concrete**				
04000	Footing contract		Lot		
04005	Building layout		Lot		
04010	Bulkhead & batterboard materials		Lot		
04015	Slag brick		Ea		
04020	#3 rebar		LF		
04025	#4 rebar		LF		
04030	#5 rebar		LF		
04035	#3 x 16" cross pieces		Ea		
04040	Tie wire		Roll		
04045	Ready-mix concrete		CY		
04050	Footing labor		Lot		
04100	Slab contract		Lot		
04105	Crushed stone (gravel)		Ton		
04110	Slag brick		Ea		
04115	#3 rebar		LF		
04120	#4 rebar		LF		
04125	#5 rebar		LF		
04130	#3 x 16" cross pieces		Ea		
04135	Tie wire		Roll		
04140	10 x 10 wire mesh (750 SF/roll)		Roll		
04145	6 mil poly		SF		
04150	6" anchor bolts, nuts, washer		Ea		
04155	Ready-mix concrete		CY		
04160	Slab labor		SF		
04300	Retaining walls		Lot		
04400	Concrete stairs & landings		Lot		
04405	10 x 10 wire mesh (750 SF/roll)		Roll		
04410	Ready-mix concrete		CY		
04415	Stairs & landings labor		SF		
04500	Lightweight concrete		Lot		
04999	Total sales tax (if applicable)				
				Total Concrete	

Figure 8-3 (cont.) Construction cost breakdown

Construction Cost Breakdown

Project Name:_____ Date:_____ Page:_____

Code	Description	Quantity	Unit	Unit Price	Extended Cost
07	**Masonry**				
07000	Concrete block contract		Lot		
07005	12" block		Ea		
07010	12" form block		Ea		
07015	8" block		Ea		
07020	8" form block		Ea		
07025	4" cap block		Ea		
07030	Slag brick		Ea		
07035	Wall ties		Box		
07040	6" anchor bolts		Ea		
07045	8" anchor bolts		Ea		
07050	Dur-O-Wal		LF		
07055	Lintels ( )		Ea		
07060	Lintels ( )		Ea		
07065	Lintels ( )		Ea		
07070	Sand		CY		
07075	Masonry mix		Bag		
07080	Lime-putty mix		CY		
07085	Drayage		Load		
07090	Block labor		Ea		
07100	Brick contract		Lot		
07105	Brick		Per M		
07110	Lintels ( )		Ea		
07115	Lintels ( )		Ea		
07120	Lintels ( )		Ea		
07125	Sand		CY		
07130	Masonry mix		Bag		
07135	Lime-putty mix		CY		
07140	Drayage		Load		
07145	Brick labor		Per M		
07200	Brick cleaning		Per M		
07999	Total sales tax (if applicable)				
				Total Masonry	

Figure 8-3 (cont.) Construction cost breakdown

Construction Cost Breakdown

Project Name:_____ Date:_____ Page:_____

Code	Description	Quantity	Unit	Unit Price	Extended Cost
10	**Metal Work**				
10000	Structural steel contract		Lot		
10100	Stairs & landings		Lot		
10200	Miscellaneous steel		Lot		
10300	Metal posts		LF		
10999	Total sales tax (if applicable)				
				Total Metal Work	

Figure 8-3 (cont.) Construction cost breakdown

Construction Cost Breakdown

Project Name:_____ Date:_____ Page:_____

Code	Description	Quantity	Unit	Unit Price	Extended Cost
13	**Rough Carpentry**				
13000	Rough carpentry contract		Lot		
13001	30# felt termite shield		Roll		
13005	2 x 6 plate		LF		
13010	2 x 4 PT plate		LF		
13015	2 x 6 PT plate		LF		
13020	2 x 4		LF		
13025	2 x 4 x 8'		Ea		
13030	2 x 4 x 10'		Ea		
13035	2 x 4 x 12'		Ea		
13040	2 x 4 x 14'		Ea		
13045	2 x 4 x 16'		Ea		
13050	2 x 4 x 18'		Ea		
13055	2 x 4 x 20'		Ea		
13060	2 x 6		LF		
13065	2 x 6 x 8'		Ea		
13070	2 x 6 x 10'		Ea		
13075	2 x 6 x 12'		Ea		
13080	2 x 6 x 14'		Ea		
13085	2 x 6 x 16'		Ea		
13090	2 x 6 x 18'		Ea		
13095	2 x 6 x 20'		Ea		
13100	2 x 6 x 22'		Ea		
13105	2 x 8		LF		
13110	2 x 8 x 8'		Ea		
13115	2 x 8 x 10'		Ea		
13120	2 x 8 x 12'		Ea		
13125	2 x 8 x 14'		Ea		
13130	2 x 8 x 16'		Ea		
13135	2 x 8 x 18'		Ea		
13140	2 x 8 x 20'		Ea		
			Subtotal Rough Carpentry		

Figure 8-3 (cont.) Construction cost breakdown

Construction Cost Breakdown

Project Name:_____   Date:_____   Page:_____

Code	Description	Quantity	Unit	Unit Price	Extended Cost
13	**Rough Carpentry continued**				
13145	2 x 10		LF		
13150	2 x 10 x 8'		Ea		
13155	2 x 10 x 10'		Ea		
13160	2 x 10 x 12'		Ea		
13165	2 x 10 x 14'		Ea		
13170	2 x 10 x 16'		Ea		
13175	2 x 10 x 18'		Ea		
13180	2 x 10 x 20'		Ea		
13185	2 x 12		LF		
13190	2 x 12 x 8'		Ea		
13195	2 x 12 x 10'		Ea		
13200	2 x 12 x 12'		Ea		
13205	2 x 12 x 14'		Ea		
13210	2 x 12 x 16'		Ea		
13215	2 x 12 x 18'		Ea		
13220	2 x 12 x 20'		Ea		
13225	5/8" T&G floor decking		Ea		
13230	¾" T&G floor decking		Ea		
13235	29 oz. tube construction glue		Ea		
13240	Utility Spruce		Ea		
13245	8' Spruce studs (nominal)		Ea		
13250	9' Spruce studs		Ea		
13255	1 x 4 x 12' corner bracing		Ea		
13260	1 x 4 attic joist bracing		LF		
13265	½" plywood corner bracing		Ea		
13270	½" Tuff-R sheathing		Ea		
13275	½" 4 x 9 Thermax sheathing		Ea		
13280	½" 4 x 9 Blackboard		Ea		
13285	½" roof decking		Ea		
	Subtotal Rough Carpentry				

Figure 8-3 (cont.) Construction cost breakdown

Construction Cost Breakdown

Project Name:_____ Date:_____ Page:_____

Code	Description	Quantity	Unit	Unit Price	Extended Cost
13	**Rough Carpentry continued**				
13290	Roof decking clips		Box		
13295	15# felt		Roll		
13300	½" particleboard		Ea		
13305	5/8" particleboard		Ea		
13310	6 mil poly		SF		
13315	8" lap siding		Pc		
13320	12" lap siding		Pc		
13325	4 x 8 siding		Pc		
13330	4 x 9 siding		Pc		
13335	1 x 6 grooved fascia		LF		
13340	1 x 2 trim		LF		
13345	3/8" AC plywood		Pc		
13350	4 x 4 x 10' hemmed flashing		Ea		
13355	Gable vent		Ea		
13360	Soffit vent		Ea		
13365	Turbine vent		Ea		
13370	Ridge vent		LF		
13375	Shutters ( )		Pr		
13380	Shutters ( )		Pr		
13385	Shutters ( )		Pr		
13390	2 x 4 PT		LF		
13395	2 x 4 x 8' PT		Ea		
13400	2 x 4 x 10' PT		Ea		
13405	2 x 4 x 12' PT		Ea		
13410	2 x 4 x 14' PT		Ea		
13415	2 x 4 x 16' PT		Ea		
13420	2 x 6 PT		LF		
13425	2 x 6 x 8' PT		Ea		
13430	2 x 6 x 10' PT		Ea		
13435	2 x 6 x 12' PT		Ea		
13440	2 x 6 x 14' PT		Ea		
13445	2 x 6 x 16' PT		Ea		
			Subtotal Rough Carpentry		

Figure 8-3 (cont.) Construction cost breakdown

Project Name:_____ Date:_____ Page:_____

Code	Description	Quantity	Unit	Unit Price	Extended Cost
13	**Rough Carpentry continued**				
13450	2 x 8 PT		LF		
13455	2 x 8 x 8' PT		Ea		
13460	2 x 8 x 10' PT		Ea		
13465	2 x 8 x 12' PT		Ea		
13470	2 x 8 x 14' PT		Ea		
13475	2 x 8 x 16' PT		Ea		
13480	2 x 10 PT		LF		
13485	2 x 10 x 8' PT		Ea		
13490	2 x 10 x 10' PT		Ea		
13495	2 x 10 x 12' PT		Ea		
13500	2 x 10 x 14' PT		Ea		
13505	2 x 10 x 16' PT		Ea		
13510	2 x 12 PT		LF		
13515	2 x 12 x 8' PT		Ea		
13520	2 x 12 x 10' PT		Ea		
13525	2 x 12 x 12' PT		Ea		
13530	2 x 12 x 14' PT		Ea		
13535	2 x 12 x 16' PT		Ea		
13540	4 x 4 x 8' PT		Ea		
13545	4 x 4 x 8' Cedar		Ea		
13550	4 x 4 x 10' PT		Ea		
13555	4 x 4 x 10' Cedar		Ea		
13560	4 x 4 x 12' PT		Ea		
13565	4 x 4 x 12' Cedar		Ea		
13570	4 x 4 x 14' PT		Ea		
13575	4 x 4 x 16' PT		Ea		
13580	6 x 6 x 8' PT		Ea		
13585	6 x 6 x 10' PT		Ea		
13590	6 x 6 x 12' PT		Ea		
13595	6 x 6 x 14' PT		Ea		
13600	6 x 6 x 16' PT		Ea		
			Subtotal Rough Carpentry		

Figure 8-3 (cont.) Construction cost breakdown

Construction Cost Breakdown

Project Name:_____ Date:_____ Page:_____

Code	Description	Quantity	Unit	Unit Price	Extended Cost
13	**Rough Carpentry continued**				
13605	8d cut nails		Box		
13610	8d sinkers		Box		
13615	8d siding nails		Box		
13620	8d galvanized sinkers		Box		
13625	8d spiral deck nails		Box		
13630	16d sinkers		Box		
13635	16d galvanized sinkers		Box		
13640	16d spiral deck nails		Box		
13645	7/8" felt cap nails		Box		
13650	1 ¾" felt cap nails		Box		
13655	7/8" roofing nails		Box		
13660	1¼" roofing nails		Box		
13665	4d galvanized box nails		Box		
13670	5" lag bolt, washer, nut		Ea		
13675	6" lag bolt, washer, nut		Ea		
13680	8" lag bolt, washer, nut		Ea		
13685	10" lag bolt, washer, nut		Ea		
13690	Rough carpentry labor		Lot		
13695	Framing labor		SF		
13700	Stairway, landings, deck labor		SF		
13800	Trusses		Lot		
13805	Roof trusses		Lot		
13810	Floor trusses		Lot		
13815	Pull down attic stairs		Ea		
13820	Miscellaneous rough carpentry labor		Lot		
	Subtotal Rough Carpentry (this page)				
13999	Total sales tax (if applicable)				
	Total Rough Carpentry				

Figure 8-3 (cont.) Construction cost breakdown

Construction Cost Breakdown

Project Name:_____   Date:_____   Page:_____

Code	Description	Quantity	Unit	Unit Price	Extended Cost
16	**Exterior Doors and Windows**				
16000	Exterior doors		Lot		
16005	2' 8" x 6' 8"-6 panel exterior door		Ea		
16010	2' 8" x 6' 8"-9 lite exterior door		Ea		
16015	2' 8" x 6' 8" French exterior door		Ea		
16020	2' 8" x 6' 8" flush exterior door		Ea		
16025	3' 0" x 6' 8"-6 panel exterior door		Ea		
16030	3' 0" x 6' 8"-9 lite exterior door		Ea		
16035	3' 0" x 6' 8" French exterior door		Ea		
16040	3' 0" x 6' 8" flush exterior door		Ea		
16045	3' 0" x 6' 8" window exterior door		Ea		
16100	Windows & screens		Lot		
16105	1' 6" x 4' 0" window & screen		Ea		
16110	1' 6" x 5' 0" window & screen		Ea		
16115	2' 0" x 3' 0" window & screen		Ea		
16120	2' 0" x 6' 2" window & screen		Ea		
16125	2' 8" x 3' 0" window & screen		Ea		
16130	2' 8" x 3' 2" window & screen		Ea		
16135	2' 8" x 4' 4" window & screen		Ea		
16140	2' 8" x 4' 4" twin window & screen		Ea		
16145	2' 8" x 4' 6" window & screen		Ea		
16150	2' 8" x 5' 0" window & screen		Ea		
16155	2' 8" x 5' 0" twin window & screen		Ea		
16160	2' 8" x 6' 2" window & screen		Ea		
16165	3' 0" x 3' 0" window & screen		Ea		
16170	3' 0" x 4' 4" window & screen		Ea		
16175	3' 0" x 5' 0" window & screen		Ea		
16200	Mull package		Ea		
16999	Total sales tax (if applicable)				
	Total Exterior Doors and Windows				

Figure 8-3 (cont.) Construction cost breakdown

Construction Cost Breakdown

Project Name:_____ Date:_____ Page:_____

Code	Description	Quantity	Unit	Unit Price	Extended Cost
19	**Plumbing**				
19000	Plumbing contract		Lot		
19100	Plumbing by builder		Lot		
19200	Septic tank & field lines		Lot		
19999	Total sales tax (if applicable)				
				Total Plumbing	

Figure 8-3 (cont.) Construction cost breakdown

Construction Cost Breakdown

Project Name:_____   Date:_____   Page:_____

Code	Description	Quantity	Unit	Unit Price	Extended Cost
22	**Electrical**				
22000	Electrical contract		Lot		
22005	Fixture allowance		Lot		
22100	Electrical by builder		Lot		
22999	Total sales tax (if applicable)				
				Total Electrical	

Figure 8-3 (cont.)   Construction cost breakdown

Construction Cost Breakdown

Project Name:_____ Date:_____ Page:_____

Code	Description	Quantity	Unit	Unit Price	Extended Cost
25	**HVAC**				
25000	HVAC contract		Lot		
25100	HVAC by builder		Lot		
25999	Total sales tax (if applicable)				
				Total HVAC	

Figure 8-3 (cont.) Construction cost breakdown

Construction Cost Breakdown

Project Name:_____   Date:_____   Page:_____

Code	Description	Quantity	Unit	Unit Price	Extended Cost
28	**Specialties**				
28000	Ceramic tile contract		Lot		
28050	Fireplace		Lot		
28100	Mirrors		Lot		
28150	Wire shelving		Lot		
28200	Termite pre-treatment		Lot		
28300	Cleaning contract		Lot		
28350	Cultured marble contract		Lot		
28400	Stucco		Lot		
28450	Drivit		Lot		
28500	Elevator		Lot		
28600	Window covering		Lot		
28605	Draperies ( )		Pr		
28610	Draperies ( )		Pr		
28615	Draperies ( )		Pr		
28650	Drapery rod ( )		Ea		
28655	Drapery rod ( )		Ea		
28660	Drapery rod ( )		Ea		
28700	Skylight		Lot		
28999	Total sales tax (if applicable)				
				Total Specialties	

Figure 8-3 (cont.)   Construction cost breakdown

Construction Cost Breakdown

Project Name:_____ Date:_____ Page:_____

Code	Description	Quantity	Unit	Unit Price	Extended Cost
31	**Insulation**				
31000	Insulation contract		Lot		
31005	R-11 wall batts		SF		
31010	R-13 wall batts		SF		
31015	R-22 blown-in insulation		SF		
31020	R-30 blown-in insulation		SF		
31100	Insulation by builder		Lot		
31999	Total sales tax (if applicable)				
				Total Insulation	

Figure 8-3 (cont.) Construction cost breakdown

Construction Cost Breakdown

Project Name:_____ Date:_____ Page:_____

Code	Description	Quantity	Unit	Unit Price	Extended Cost
34	**Moisture Protection**				
34000	Roofing contract		Lot		
34005	240# 3-tab shingles		Sq		
34010	7/8" roofing nails		Box		
34015	1¼" roofing nails		Box		
34020	Valley tin		LF		
34025	Roofing labor		Sq		
34100	Sheet metal		Lot		
34300	Gutter & downspout contract		Lot		
34305	Gutters		LF		
34310	Downspouts		LF		
34315	Splash blocks		Ea		
34320	Drain piping		LF		
34325	Gutters & downspouts labor		Lot		
34400	Waterproofing (foundation)		Lot		
34405	Drain piping		LF		
34410	Gravel		Ton		
34999	Total sales tax (if applicable)				
	Total Moisture Protection				

Figure 8-3 (cont.) Construction cost breakdown

Construction Cost Breakdown

Project Name:_____ Date:_____ Page:_____

Code	Description	Quantity	Unit	Unit Price	Extended Cost
37	**Drywall**				
37000	Drywall contract		Lot		
37005	5/8" 4 x 12 firerock		Ea		
37010	5/8" 4 x 8 firerock		Ea		
37015	5/8" 4 x 10 firerock		Ea		
37020	5/8" 4-1/2 x 12 drywall		Ea		
37025	½" 4 x 12 drywall		Ea		
37030	½" 4 x 8 drywall		Ea		
37035	5/8" 4 x 8 moisture resistant		Ea		
37040	5/8" 4 x 8 firewalls		Ea		
37045	5/8" 4 x 8 smokewalls		Ea		
37100	Drywall labor		SF		
37999	Total sales tax (if applicable)				
				Total Drywall	

Figure 8-3 (cont.) Construction cost breakdown

Construction Cost Breakdown

Project Name:_____ Date:_____ Page:_____

Code	Description	Quantity	Unit	Unit Price	Extended Cost
40	**Cabinets & Countertops**				
40000	Cabinet contract		Lot		
40100	Cabinets by builder		Lot		
40999	Total sales tax (if applicable)				
	Total Cabinets & Countertops				

Figure 8-3 (cont.) Construction cost breakdown

Construction Cost Breakdown

Project Name:_____ Date:_____ Page:_____

Code	Description	Quantity	Unit	Unit Price	Extended Cost
43	**Finish Carpentry**				
43000	Finish carpentry contract		Lot		
43005	Baseboard		LF		
43010	Casing		LF		
43015	Window stool		LF		
43020	Shoe mold		LF		
43025	6' plastic corner mold		Ea		
43030	Crown mold		LF		
43035	Quarter round		LF		
43040	Chair rail		LF		
43045	Shelving		LF		
43050	1 x 4 Spruce		LF		
43055	1 x 6 Spruce		LF		
43060	4d finish nails		Lb		
43065	6d finish nails		Lb		
43070	8d finish nails		Lb		
43075	Fireplace mantel		Lot		
43080	Finish carpentry labor		Lot		
43100	Interior door contract		Lot		
43105	1' 6" x 6' 8" interior doors		Ea		
43110	2' 0" x 6' 8" interior doors		Ea		
43115	2' 4" x 6' 8" interior doors		Ea		
43120	2' 6" x 6' 8" interior doors		Ea		
43130	2' 8" x 6' 8" interior doors		Ea		
43135	3' 0" x 6' 8" interior doors		Ea		
43140	4' 0" x 6' 8" interior dbl. hung doors		Ea		
43150	Interior door labor		Lot		
43200	Interior stairs contract		Lot		
43205	Handrail		Ea		
43210	Pickets		Ea		
43215	Newel post		Ea		
43220	Fillets		Ea		
43225	Rosettes		Ea		
43250	Interior stair labor		Lot		
43999	Total sales tax (if applicable)				
	Total Finish Carpentry				

Figure 8-3 (cont.) Construction cost breakdown

Project Name:_____ Date:_____ Page:_____

Code	Description	Quantity	Unit	Unit Price	Extended Cost
46	**Finish Hardware**				
46000	Finish hardware contract		Lot		
46001	18" towel rod		Ea		
46005	24" towel rod		Ea		
46010	Shower curtain rod		Ea		
46015	Paper holder		Ea		
46020	Medicine cabinet		Ea		
46025	Shelf bracket		Ea		
46030	14" x 14" air vent		Ea		
46035	Closet rod ( )		Ea		
46040	Closet rod ( )		Ea		
46045	Closet rod ( )		Ea		
46050	Door stop		Ea		
46060	Handrail bracket		Ea		
46065	Door numbers		Ea		
46070	Mail boxes		Ea		
46100	Locks & knobs		Lot		
46105	Single cylinder deadbolt		Ea		
46110	Double cylinder deadbolt		Ea		
46115	Keyed knob		Ea		
46120	Privacy knob		Ea		
46125	Passage knob		Ea		
46130	Dummy knob		Ea		
46150	Locks & knobs labor		Lot		
46160	Keys		Ea		
46999	Total sales tax (if applicable)				
				Total Finish Hardware	

Figure 8-3 (cont.) Construction cost breakdown

Construction Cost Breakdown

Project Name:_____ Date:_____ Page:_____

Code	Description	Quantity	Unit	Unit Price	Extended Cost
49	**Painting & Wallpaper**				
49000	Painting contract		Lot		
49001	Painting materials		Lot		
49005	Painting labor		Lot		
49100	Wallpaper contract		Lot		
49105	Wallpaper materials		Lot		
49110	Wallpaper labor		Lot		
49999	Total sales tax (if applicable)				
	Total Painting & Wallpaper				

Figure 8-3 (cont.) Construction cost breakdown

Construction Cost Breakdown

Project Name:_____ Date:_____ Page:_____

Code	Description	Quantity	Unit	Unit Price	Extended Cost
52	**Exterior Flatwork & Paving**				
52000	Flatwork & paving contract		Lot		
52005	Forming materials		Lot		
52010	Ready-mix concrete		CY		
52015	Asphalt spacers		LF		
52020	10 x 10 wire mesh (750 SF/roll)		Roll		
52025	Exterior flatwork labor		Lot		
52100	Concrete curbs & gutters		LF		
52200	Asphalt paving		SY		
52300	Parking & traffic controls		Lot		
52305	Car bumpers		Ea		
52310	Striping		Lot		
52315	Bumper & striping labor		Lot		
52999	Total sales tax (if applicable)				
	Total Exterior Flatwork & Paving				

Figure 8-3 (cont.)   Construction cost breakdown

Construction Cost Breakdown

Project Name:_____ Date:_____ Page:_____

Code	Description	Quantity	Unit	Unit Price	Extended Cost
55	**Flooring**				
55000	Flooring contract		Lot		
55005	Carpet		SY		
55010	Vinyl		SY		
55015	Tile		SY		
55020	Wood flooring		SF		
55999	Total sales tax (if applicable)				
				Total Flooring	

Figure 8-3 (cont.) Construction cost breakdown

Construction Cost Breakdown

Project Name:_____ Date:_____ Page:_____

Code	Description	Quantity	Unit	Unit Price	Extended Cost
58	**Appliances**				
58000	Kitchen appliances		Lot		
58005	Range		Ea		
58010	Range hood		Ea		
58015	Refrigerator		Ea		
58020	Dishwasher		Ea		
58025	Garbage disposal		Ea		
58030	Microwave oven		Ea		
58035	Trash compactor		Ea		
58100	Laundry room equipment		Lot		
58105	Washing machine		Ea		
58110	Dryer		Ea		
58200	Appliance delivery		Lot		
58999	Total sales tax (if applicable)				
				Total Appliances	

Figure 8-3 (cont.) Construction cost breakdown

Construction Cost Breakdown

Project Name:_____ Date:_____ Page:_____

Code	Description	Quantity	Unit	Unit Price	Extended Cost
61	**Landscaping**				
61000	Landscaping contract		Lot		
61005	Landscaping by builder		Lot		
61100	Fencing		Lot		
61999	Total sales tax (if applicable)				
				Total Landscaping	

Figure 8-3 (cont.) Construction cost breakdown

Construction Cost Breakdown

Project Name:_____ Date:_____ Page:_____

Code	Description	Quantity	Unit	Unit Price	Extended Cost
64	**Furnishings & Equipment**				
64000	Furnishings & equipment contract		Lot		
64005	Recreation structures & equipment		Lot		
64010	Other structures & equipment		Lot		
64015	Furniture		Lot		
64020	Pool		Lot		
64100	Equipment delivery		Lot		
64999	Total sales tax (if applicable)				
	Total Furnishings & Equipment				

Figure 8-3 (cont.) Construction cost breakdown

Construction Cost Breakdown

Project Name:_____ Date:_____ Page:_____

Code	Description	Quantity	Unit	Unit Price	Extended Cost
67	**Salaries, Wages, Fees**				
67000	Salaries, wages, fees		Lot		
67005	Miscellaneous labor		Lot		
67010	Superintendent		Mo		
67015	Security services		Lot		
67020	Administrative		Lot		
67999	Total sales tax (if applicable)				
			Total Salaries, Wages, Fees		

Figure 8-3 (cont.)   Construction cost breakdown

Construction Cost Breakdown

Project Name:_____ Date:_____ Page:_____

Code	Description	Quantity	Unit	Unit Price	Extended Cost
70	**Equipment Costs**				
70000	Equipment costs		Lot		
70005	Scaffolding		Lot		
70010	Material hoisting		Lot		
70015	Miscellaneous equipment & tools		Lot		
70020	Truck & transportation		Lot		
70025	Concrete pump		Lot		
70030	Temporary fence		Lot		
70035	Dumpster		Lot		
70045	Temporary toilet		Mo		
70999	Total sales tax (if applicable)				
				Total Equipment Costs	

Figure 8-3 (cont.)   Construction cost breakdown

Construction Cost Breakdown

Project Name:_____   Date:_____   Page:_____

Code	Description	Quantity	Unit	Unit Price	Extended Cost
73	**Utility Costs**				
73000	Utility costs		Lot		
73005	Temporary electricity		Mo		
73010	Temporary water		Mo		
73015	Temporary phone		Mo		
73999	Total sales tax (if applicable)				
				Total Utility Costs	

Figure 8-3 (cont.) Construction cost breakdown

Construction Cost Breakdown

Project Name:_____   Date:_____   Page:_____

Code	Description	Quantity	Unit	Unit Price	Extended Cost
76	**Miscellaneous Job Costs**				
76000	Miscellaneous job costs		Lot		
76005	Field office		Lot		
76010	Storage costs		Lot		
76015	Job signs		Lot		
76020	Access roadwork		Lot		
76025	Insurance		Lot		
76999	Total sales tax (if applicable)				
	Total Miscellaneous Job Costs				

Figure 8-3 (cont.)   Construction cost breakdown

Chapter 9
Estimating Construction Costs

In this chapter I'll explain how to develop the costs you list on the construction cost breakdown (Figure 8-3 starting on page 108). As you read this chapter, you'll probably want to refer back to Figure 8-3 from time to time.

The construction cost breakdown form assumes you have two types of job costs. Every job cost is either a subcontract cost or a combination of labor and material costs.

Notice that on the construction cost breakdown, all costs that are subcontracted have the same entry in the units column: "Lot." Any work that's performed by a subcontractor is charged to you as a lump sum. Here's how it works. Each bidding subcontractor quotes you a single price covering the whole job. That means all costs for labor and materials as per your specifications. That figure also includes the subcontractor's overhead and profit.

Spec home builders almost always subcontract, at the absolute minimum, installation of the following major systems:

- Plumbing
- Electrical
- HVAC (heating, ventilation, air conditioning)

Common sense and the building inspector require these systems to be installed by licensed professionals.

Most spec builders also subcontract other work. That's especially the case for those jobs that require a specialist's skills or equipment. For example:

- Cabinetry
- Insulation
- Landscaping
- Metal work
- Ceramic tile
- Roofing

Flooring

 Final cleaning

The rest of the construction work you'll hire out to tradesmen or to a contractor. In either case, the contractor (or tradesman) provides his own labor, his crews, and tools. You'll buy and furnish the materials required. Framing, masonry, drywall and concrete work are usually done on this basis.

Obviously, there's no need for you to estimate costs on any of the subcontract work. All you do is give several subcontractors copies of your plans and specs, answer their questions, and record the figures when they submit their bids.

Two Steps in Every Estimate

No matter who does the estimating, there are two parts to every construction cost estimate: the quantity take-off, and then the pricing.

Step One

A quantity take-off (sometimes called a quantity survey) is counting and calculating. How much lumber? How many cubic yards of concrete? How many doors and windows? The estimator tries to determine, by reading the plans and specifications, the quantity and type of materials and equipment needed to complete the job. I'm sure you understand how very important details are to a material quantity estimate. Even the simplest home has hundreds and hundreds of cost items. Identifying every single one is very important. Otherwise the estimate won't be accurate. Generally, the quantity take-off is about 80 percent of the estimator's task.

There are two times when you'll use the information from the quantity take-off: When you price the job, and when you order the material. Because you use these numbers twice, any mistake you make in a quantity take-off will hurt twice. For starters, your estimated costs are wrong. Later on, at the job site, the amount of material delivered is too much or not enough.

The Second Step

When the quantity take-off is complete, pricing can begin. The estimator determines the most likely cost for each item listed in the quantity take-off. This is seldom, if ever, as easy as it may sound. Costs vary because no two jobs are exactly the same. Then there's the matter of lag time. Weeks pass between the time that you finish an estimate and the time that the work starts. Sometimes even months go by. It's not easy to anticipate conditions so far in the future.

Once you've made your unit cost estimates (per door, per square foot of drywall, per square foot of roof, for example) the next order of business is to extend these costs. That's easy, because all you do is multiply the unit cost by the number of units. For example, if roofing shingles are $40 per 100 square feet and you need

1600 square feet, the extended cost for shingles is equal to $40 times 16, or $640. Notice that the construction cost breakdown form includes a column for recording these figures.

To find the total cost for a category, add up all the extended cost figures within the category. To find the total construction cost, add all the category totals.

Beginning a Quantity Survey

Your first step is to decide which portions of the project to sub out to specialty contractors and which to handle yourself. Most spec builders get subcontract bids from plumbing, electrical and HVAC contractors. Those are easy decisions. You can delay decisions on some subcontract items, such as landscaping. Just make an initial rough estimate for now. When the building is nearing completion, get bids on exterior flatwork, paving, sprinklers and other exterior improvements.

There's good reason to delay soliciting bids on some work (such as the landscaping) that won't be required for several months. The more risk and uncertainty you can take out of a job, the more competitive a subcontractor's price is likely to be. If the subcontractor can see exactly what's needed and when, his estimate won't include allowances for unknowns and contingencies. The result — you get a more realistic bid. If you ask for bids too soon, you'll probably get what we call "courtesy bids." Typically the figures in a courtesy bid are very high. That's because the subcontractor knows that the job may never actually materialize.

I recommend that you prepare your own quantity take-offs. The yellow pages in most metropolitan area phone books have several listings for professional quantity surveyor firms. Pay them a fee and they'll provide you with a quantity take-off based on the plans. However, I don't recommend it. The issue here isn't the cost. Rather, it's the inherent value that mastering the plans has for you. By doing your own estimating and pricing, you become intimately familiar with every last item that's going into your spec home. It essentially forces you to construct the whole house in your mind. Do that and you're sure to spot errors while there's still plenty of time to correct them.

That's not the only reason I recommend doing your own quantity take-off. Remember you need to watch your expenses like a hawk. Nobody else has the incentive you do to look for every possible best price. There's nothing like doing a cost take-off for making you cost-conscious.

Take-off Procedures

Material take-offs aren't difficult to do. But they do take time, care and attention to detail. The key is taking it one step at a time. Start with the site work and then simply follow the order of construction. Most of the necessary calculations involve simple math. I'll be covering all of this in detail later on in the chapter.

A quantity take-off does require some special skills. For one thing, every contractor I know would rather be at work on a construction site than sitting at an office desk figuring an estimate. That's probably because most contractors are better at construction than at estimating. Knowledge of construction is helpful to the estimator, of course, but construction skills aren't the same as estimating skills. Having a talent for construction doesn't necessarily mean you'll find estimating a piece of cake.

Good estimators do their work in a very systematic way. A little disorganization will turn what should have been an elementary procedure into a nightmare. So estimators follow a regular set of procedures and routines from beginning to end. You'll soon find that take-offs are both easier and quicker to do once you have a system. Try following the one I'll outline in the rest of this chapter. Use it with the construction cost breakdown (Figure 8-3) at the end of Chapter 8. Together they should considerably lighten your estimating burden.

Finding Good Contractors and Suppliers

Where do you find the best subcontractors and material suppliers? The yellow pages in your phone directory probably include pages of listings for subs in every trade. That, however, is not a route I use or recommend. Many of these companies may not have been active for a year or more. Some may even be incompetent, dishonest or worse. There *is* a better way. My experience has convinced me that the best subs are also the busiest. For my money, the best way to find good subs is to visit other projects similar in size and character to what you're planning. This rule also holds true when it comes to finding the best tradesmen and suppliers.

Trucks parked on a job site often have the names (as well as addresses and phone numbers) of the subcontractor painted on the doors. If that's not the case, there's nothing wrong with asking the builder or superintendent for this information. If they don't happen to be available, just ask one of the tradesman. Superintendents are usually glad to supply you with the names and phone numbers of their subs. By passing on such information they're giving not only a future job referral but also an endorsement. This wins them points with their subs.

Don't get carried away though. Be casual. Limit your inquiries to one or two trades at a time. There's no need to go through your entire shopping list. A little encouragement and you'll probably also get the names of the subs who bid the job and didn't get it. If the superintendent is stonewalling you it doesn't mean you're out of luck. Bide your time and catch one of the subs when he's on his lunch break. Once you've invited bids from a few of the busiest subcontractors, getting referrals for subs in other trades gets easier. Typically, the best subcontractors in each different trade know each other and find themselves working together job after job.

Getting the Best Price - Once you've developed a bidders' list, there are several things you'll want them all to understand.

1) Impress on all the bidders just how *very* serious you are about prices. Leave no room for doubt on this score. The job goes to the lowest *responsive and responsible* bidder, period. All things being equal (although they seldom are), the low man is the one who gets your business.

2) Make it very clear that you're not just shopping around. You aren't checking out prices for a "maybe" or a "someday" project. You are *absolutely* serious about building.

"Well, they were the low bidder."

3) Explain to everyone that you expect their first bid to be their last bid on a job. There isn't going to be any after-the-fact negotiating.

4) Tell everyone right up-front that you don't believe in what's called "bid shopping." What you're saying here is this: You won't show any bids you receive to competing bidders until after the job's awarded.

I realize that many builders don't work this way. But I do and I always will. Believe you me, this policy saves me a lot of time and more than a little embarrassment. Practices such as bid shopping (showing a bidder his competitors' quotes) are all too common in the construction industry. However, like most shady deals, bid shopping has its own somewhat dubious reward. There's nothing like it for cutting a good reputation out from under a builder.

Rules Are Made to Be Broken - Sometimes, I *choose* to ignore my own rules. This one for instance: "The job goes to the lowest responsive and responsible bidder." So why would I want to ignore my own advice and award a job to a sub who didn't turn in the lowest bid? There are times when I feel it's in my best interests to pay a bit extra and break my own rules. Let me explain what I mean with an example.

Suppose Company (or supplier) A submits a bid that's about $100 higher than Company B's bid on the same job. The total price quoted for the job in both bids is about $3,000. Now let's add the fact that I've worked with Company A on several earlier projects. I have every confidence in him and his crews. Their ability to deliver a good product on schedule is a proven fact. Company B, however, is completely unknown to me. I've never worked with them before. Company B is new to the area and none of my associates can tell me much about them. What should I do? Who should get the work? What would you do?

Remember the difference between the two bids is only $100. What to do? I'd give the job to Company A. Sometimes it's smart to pay a little extra. In a situation like this I'd consider that $100 to be money well spent. Here's why. There's always some risk involved in working with a new or unknown subcontractor. Is the workmanship up to your standards? What about your schedule; will this company manage to meet your deadlines? If I can completely avoid the risk for just $100 I think it's worth it.

There's only one drawback involved here. That's explaining my choice to Company B. I believe that honesty's the best policy at times like this. I just grit my teeth and call my contact at Company B. I'll briefly explain what I've done and why, while trying to avoid burning bridges. I make it clear that I'm willing to switch subs on the next job. I also make a point of explaining just how narrow the margin of difference was that lost them the job. I imply that using a little sharper pencil on their next bid will probably land them the job. I don't expect a session like this to win me any friends at company B. I count it as a success if I sense that there's no ill will when I hang up. Sometimes you'll even find that people appreciate your candor — but don't count on it.

Now let's look at how I decide whether the price difference between close bids is worth the risk involved. I've found it helpful in these cases to look at the difference as a percentage of the total price quoted. In this example the difference between bids is $100. The total price quoted by both parties is about $3,000. And 100 divided by 3,000 is 0.033, or 3.3 percent. Not much, is it? Now watch what happens if nothing changes except the difference between the two bids. This time Company B submits a bid that's $600 lower than Company A's bid. Now 600 divided by 3,000 is 0.20, or 20 percent. In my book that's a whole different ball game. For 20 percent I'd probably accept the risk of giving the job to Company B.

Bids and Bidders With "The Right Stuff" - Earlier I used the phrase *responsive and responsible* to describe what I look for in subcontractors and their bids. I recommended awarding the work to the "lowest responsive and responsible bidder." That's not just a fancy name for the lowest bidder. In the context of a construction work bid, both "responsive" and "responsible" have *very* specific meanings which we'll discuss in detail. You, the spec builder, have the right to ignore any bid or bidder that fails the "responsive and responsible" test.

Responsive bids and bidders: A *responsive* bid is one that's based precisely on the plans and specs you provide. A responsive bidder doesn't add or change any part of your specs or plans. Any time the bid assumes a change or a bidder imposes their own qualifications you're not, I repeat *not,* dealing with a responsive bidder. Turning in a nonresponsive bid is like answering a question with a question. Bids that aren't responsive are a waste of your time. Never feel obliged to accept one. You can't make a true comparison between bids unless they're all based on exactly the same plans and specs. You'd be trying to compare apples to oranges — it can't be done.

Vendors and subs know this as well as anyone. Most of them are honest businessmen like you, but once in a while you may run into a bad apple. They'll do their worst, but don't let these shysters bamboozle you. Everything they suggest is "required" either by "the code" or "good construction practices." Why would anyone go to such lengths? It's simple greed! If you adopt their change, all the other bids are for the wrong job. You're stuck with these guys now and guess who's running the show?

Don't get me wrong though. I'm not saying that all vendors and subs are no better than crooks. As I said, most of them are good honest businessmen. Every change that's suggested isn't a trap. Keep an open mind. Often changes that subs or vendors suggest can save you money or time or enhance a spec home's quality. Just be sure to weigh the value of any change against the potential headaches.

I recommend that you treat this the way that I do. Say that a trusted sub or vendor suggests a change in my plans or specs. I ask them to bid the work twice. Tell them to send you one bid that follows the plans and specs you sent out. Then say you'll be glad to look at a second bid that assumes making the recommended change or changes. This is a win-win situation for you. You have a comparable bid *and* some useful advice. After you receive the bid, there's time to consider the suggestions and make clear-headed choices.

Responsible bidders: Although a low price is important to you, it's not all that you'll want to consider. Pay attention to who's quoting you a price for what job. You're sure to run into lots of repair and remodeling contractors who bid on work that's much larger than anything they've ever done before. They're experimenting and testing their limits. That's good, for them. But they shouldn't test themselves at your expense. You don't have to be a guinea pig and accept the risk of their failing.

If you have reason to suspect a bidder's integrity or capabilities, ask for references or a list of jobs completed — preferably before the bids are submitted. This is known as "qualifying the bidders." I always do this when I'm dealing with a new firm. It's a good business practice that I urge you to follow. Here's a rule of thumb: Never let a sub you wouldn't want to sign a contract with submit a bid. That's just common courtesy. Make a special point of getting references ahead of time. It's the best way to avoid a dilemma I've run into several times: The most attractive bid is from a Johnny-come-lately who has few (if any) references and very little experience. Accepting this bid is a pure crapshoot.

Spec building carries enough inherent risks already. There's certainly no reason to take on additional and unnecessary chances. That's why I recommend you request bids only from responsible, responsive bidders. Then you can base your final decision solely (or almost solely) on price.

The Value of Specifications

You need to supply each subcontractor with a full set of plans and specs before they bid on the work. The plans, of course, were prepared by your designer. Your designer may also be able to provide a list of standard specifications that comply with the local building code.

I prefer to use my own specifications. Take a look at Figure 9-1. This is a package of specifications that covers each of the trades or work categories. I've used these successfully many times, after adjusting them to fit my current project. But that's a personal choice that you may or may not choose to follow. Here's the way I see it. I honestly don't feel it's helpful to anyone to include details beyond what's absolutely necessary in the specs. However, there are other points of view. Some spec builders I know firmly believe that the longer the specifications, the better. They feel that by spelling out every single detail in long specifications they're

HOME BUILDER'S CONSTRUCTION COMPANY
621 Randolph Road
Newport News, VA 23605
(012) 555-6789

STANDARD SPECIFICATIONS AND PROCEDURES

GENERAL CONDITIONS: All specs to be same, or equal.

■ All "equal" are subject to approval by builder.

■ All contractors to provide Certificates of Insurance for Workers' Compensation and liability insurance.

Please return plans and a *signed* copy of the specifications with your quote.

01 SITE WORK

SITE WORK (BEFORE CONSTRUCTION)   The site will be cleared and brought to rough grade. No other clearing or grubbing is allowed, except with the isolated incidence of dangerous dead tree removal.

SITE WORK (AFTER CONSTRUCTION)   Grading will be as close as possible to the levels specified by the site plan while providing positive water drainage from the site. It is understood that adjustments in grade may be necessary due to the topography and the layout of adjacent property.

04 CONCRETE

FOUNDATIONS   Bearing soil is clay gravel, either natural state or compacted to at least 95% standard Proctor density in fill areas. Foundations shall consist of poured concrete footings of 3,000 PSI ready-mix, with reinforcement as required by code; concrete block walls and piers. Foundation vents to be provided as required. Crawl space to be covered with 6 mil polyethylene membrane.

SLAB CONSTRUCTION   Slab concrete shall be 4" thick and made using 3,000 PSI ready-mix. 1/2" x 4" asphalt expansion joint(s) to be provided at all joints between concrete and header blocks, if such joints are detailed. Slab to be slick finished.

07 MASONRY

FOUNDATION WALLS   Any required foundation or retaining walls to be as detailed on the plans. All such walls shall be brick veneer or stucco finish over concrete block as per plans.

BRICK   All brick shall be regular sized (St. Marie, Dorchester, or equal) as supplied by Hampton Brick & Block. Mortar and brick style and color as per Decorator.

10 METAL WORK

All metal to be prime coated.

Figure 9-1   Sample of standard specifications and procedures

13 ROUGH CARPENTRY

LUMBER   All wood sills and plates in direct contact with concrete, masonry, or steel shall be pressure treated #2 SYP.

All sole plates shall be pressure treated 2 x 4 #2 SYP or Spruce STDBTR.

All top plates shall be 2 x 4 utility, West Coast species or Spruce STDBTR.

Subflooring to be ¾" T&G plywood.

All studs shall be pre-cut spruce studs, spaced 16' o.c. 2 x 4 x 9' (1st floor) and 2 x 4 x 8' (2nd floor).

All headers shall be 2 x 10 #2 SYP or Spruce STDBTR for all loadbearing walls and 2 x 4 West Coast Species or Spruce for non-loadbearing walls.

All joists shall be #2 SYP, or West Coast species spaced as per plans.

All hips, valley and ridges shall be 2 x 8 SYP.

All rafters shall be 2 x 6 #2 SYP or Spruce STDBTR, spaced 24" o.c.

Insulating sheathing shall be ½" x 4' x 9' foam insulation board, Celotex "Tuff-R" or equal, for brick areas; or ½" x 4' x 8' exterior grade GYP sheathing for Dryvit areas.

On zero-lot line side of units utilizing Dryvit, exterior sheathing to be ⅝" fire-rated to comply with a one-hour fire wall rating.

Bracing material to be as follows:

Corners - ½" x 4' x 9' CDX plywood or OSB Board (Solid).

Bridging - Solid 2 x 10 #2 SYP.

Strongbacks - 2 x 6 #2 SYP.

Roof deck shall be ½" CDX 4-ply plywood with clips or OSB Board with clips covered with 15# felt.

All fascia shall be 1 x 6 spruce or finger jointed cedar.

All horizontal soffit material shall be ⅜" a/c plywood with continuous screened cornice vents or 8" x 16" eave vents.

All exterior exposed siding shall be Masonite "Superside" or equal, 6" smooth lap siding.

Stair stringers and treads to be 2 x 12 #2 SYP. Stair risers to be 1 x 8 #2 SYP on finished stairs.

PROCEDURES FOR FRAMING CONTRACTORS

1) Framing Contractor to provide and pay for all hoisting equipment, crane, scaffolding and tools required to perform the work contracted for herein.

2) All carpentry must conform to the Uniform Building Code and local building codes and any non-compliance shall be repaired and/or replaced by Framing Contractor at his expense.

3) Framing Contractor is responsible for installing all rough carpentry lumber including but not limited to the following: exterior doors and windows, gable vents and screening on same, soffit vents, turbine vents, roofing felt, semi-rigid insulation board, Masonite siding, metal posts, trusses and flashing.

4) Framing Contractor is responsible for hoisting trusses.

Figure 9-1 (cont.)   Sample of standard specifications and procedures

5) Framing Contractor is responsible for all wood blocking for surface mounted materials, i.e. bath accessories, lights, etc. Framing Contractor must verify locations of all wood blocking with Builder prior to installation.

6) All requests for materials must be scheduled and coordinated with Builder at least twenty-four (24) hours prior to required delivery time.

7) Exterior doors must be set plumb and aligned so as to preclude the presence of any air gaps between door and jamb. Wood shims between jamb and stud walls are required with a minimum of three (3) shims on each side and one (1) shim at head. A minimum of one (1) three-inch (3") wood screw is required for each hinge plate.

16 EXTERIOR DOORS AND WINDOWS

EXTERIOR DOORS   All front doors shall be 6 panel insulated "Therma-Tru" metal doors as provided by Norfolk Sash & Door Co., or equal. Each door shall be bored for keyed lock and single cylinder deadbolt.

All patio doors shall be one (1) lite "Therma-Tru" metal insulated French doors as supplied by Norfolk Sash & Door, or equal.

EXTERIOR WINDOWS   All windows shall be double hung "Arma-Seal" wood insulated with full screens as manufactured by Norfolk Sash & Door or equal. Sizes and layouts of windows detailed in plans.

19 PLUMBING

KITCHEN   Sink - Dayton Kingsford #K-23322 with Delta 400 fixture and sprayer.

Dishwasher connection, disposal connection and ice maker line to refrigerator space.

MASTER BATH   1 36" x 60" or 36" x 72" (see plans) cultured marble garden tub with deck mounted Delta #2710 fixtures.

1 Elger elongated commode #091-0150, or equal.

Cultured marble lavatory countertop and bowls with Delta #522 MPU chrome fixtures.

1 job built cultured marble shower with Delta 636 chrome fixtures.

2ND BATH   1 Elger elongated commode #091-0150, or equal.

1 Elger #201-1420 white cast iron tub, or equal, with Delta #636 chrome fixtures.

Cultured marble lavatory countertop and bowls with Delta #522 MPU chrome fixtures.

WATER HEATER   RUDD #P40-7, natural gas fired, 40 gallon unit, standard efficiency.

OTHER   Washer and dryer connections also included with dryer vented to the outside.

Drain waste vents in main trunk to be 4" PVC, vent stacks to be 2" and 3" PVC.

PROCEDURES FOR PLUMBING CONTRACTORS

1) Plumbing Contractor is responsible for all costs associated with cutting and paving streets or alleys and connecting to water and sewer mains. Check with Builder on location of street cut.

2) Plumbing Contractor to talk with Builder prior to framing regarding furring, enlarging walls, etc.

Figure 9-1 (cont.)   Sample of standard specifications and procedures

3) Plumbing Contractor to supply all plumbing fixtures except:

   a) Dishwasher

   b) Cultured marble lavatories

   c) Cultured marble tub and shower

4) Owner to pay sewer impact fees.

5) Plumbing Contractor to purchase water meter loop and pay for water tap.

6) Plumbing Contractor to provide all materials and labor for gas piping according to code.

7) Plumbing Contractor to install two (2) outside water faucets (talk with Builder as to faucet and cut-off locations).

8) Sewer and water to be run on or before rough carpentry inspection.

9) Talk with Builder regarding clean-out and main cut-off locations.

10) Plumbing Contractor to supply and install fixtures (except those provided by Builder) as per above specs.

11) Plumbing Contractor to run gas to log lighter in fireplace.

---

22 ELECTRICAL

Service cable shall be aluminum.

Main service to be 200 amp.

All internal house wiring shall be copper as follows:

Switches and receptacles - #14 wire.

Kitchen and Utility - #12 wire.

PROCEDURES FOR ELECTRICAL CONTRACTORS

1) Electrical Contractor to install and connect ranges.

2) Electrical Contractor to supply and install:

   a) Three (3) phone outlets

   b) Three (3) cable-TV outlets

   c) Two (2) double floods (location to be discussed with Builder)

3) Electrical Contractor responsible for temporary power and power pole.

4) Builder to supply range hood, dishwasher, disposal and microwave. Electrical Contractor to connect.

5) Electrical Contractor to install AC smoke detectors according to code requirements.

6) Electrical Contractor to handle electrical service requirements with Power Company if necessary.

7) Electrical Contractor to handle telephone service requirements with Telephone Company if necessary.

8) Electrical Contractor to install light bulbs in all fixtures.

9) Builder to pay for and supply all fixtures as per list provided by Decorator. Electrical Contractor to pick-up from supplier of Builder's choice all fixtures and install same as per list provided by Decorator.

Figure 9-1 (cont.)   Sample of standard specifications and procedures

10) Electrical Contractor is responsible for assembly and installation of ceiling fans.

11) All electrical work shall meet the requirements of the National Electrical Code.

12) All appurtenance plates shall be ivory in color.

25 HVAC

EQUIPMENT   Split unit - Electric air, gas heat - Carrier, or equal.

Thermostat - Carrier, or equal.

PROCEDURES FOR HVAC CONTRACTORS

1) HVAC Contractor to discuss capacity of HVAC unit(s) with Builder prior to starting work.

2) HVAC Contractor to provide concrete pads for condensing unit(s).

3) HVAC Contractor responsible for dryer vent and trim around dryer vent.

4) HVAC Contractor to provide venting pipe for vented bathroom fans.

5) HVAC Contractor responsible for low voltage wiring to HVAC units.

6) Location of thermostat(s) to be discussed with Builder.

7) Filter of standard size to be installed either in return grille(s) or on HVAC unit. If installed on HVAC unit filters to be installed in such a manner and location as to facilitate easy changing of filters. Filter removal and replacement to be unrestricted by condensate lines, electrical wiring, drains, etc. The filter, if installed on the HVAC unit, is to be located on the unit's exterior and installed in such a way that the filter may easily slide in and out of the filter slot without requiring any use of tools.

8) HVAC Contractor to discuss with Builder placement of condensate units.

9) All penetrations through exterior walls shall be patched and sealed in a manner satisfactory to Builder.

10) HVAC Contractor to provide minimum clearances of two feet (2') on all sides of condensing units.

28 SPECIALTIES

TERMITE PRETREATMENT   The foundation area will be pretreated for termites by a State-licensed Exterminating Company utilizing the required chemicals for effective treatment, as required by and in compliance with local building codes. A renewable one-year bond will be provided.

CERAMIC TILE   As per Decorator instructions for installation in the following areas:

■ *Master Bath:* Floor, Base

■ *2nd Bath:* Floor, Base

WIRE SHELVING   All shelving shall be vinyl-coated wire shelving located and installed as detailed on plans and as per Decorator's instructions.

FIREPLACE   Majestic MBU-36 non-circulating to be located in the Living Room and without outside air kit or heat circulator. Wire pull screen shall be provided as part of the prefabricated fireplace. Gas log lighter to be included.

Figure 9-1 (cont.)   Sample of standard specifications and procedures

No glass doors or special screens are to be provided with fireplace. Fireplace is to sit on the floor with a flat hearth. Hearth to be approximately 16" to 20" deep and a minimum of 48" wide.

Chimney to be determined.

CULTURED MARBLE   As per Decorator's instructions to be installed in the following areas:

- *Master Bath:* 1 (one) marble tub and shower, 1 (one) bath vanity top with 4" backsplash
- *2nd Bath:* 1 (one) bathtub surround to 7' above finished floor, 1 (one) bath vanity top with 4" backsplash

SHOWER ENCLOSURE   Clear glass shower enclosure with one out-swinging door in master bath. Trim to be chrome.

---

31 INSULATION

CEILING   Insulation above ceilings in attic space areas shall be either loose-fill fiberglass or rock wool and shall provide a insulation value of R-30. Insulation shall be installed so as to result in a blanket of even depth throughout the affected attic space. If required, ceiling insulation in slope ceilings (where insulation may not be blown) shall be R-19 batt insulation.

Under attic flooring insulation, where applicable, shall be R-19 batt insulation.

EXTERIOR WALLS   All exterior walls shall receive batt or roll insulation of a thickness to be equal to the nominal thickness of the wall. Insulation in standard 2 x 4 stud walls to be 3½" thick and to carry an insulating value of R-11.

FLOORS (IF CRAWL SPACE)   All 1st level floors shall receive batt insulation 3½" thick and carry an insulating value of R-11.

BATHROOMS   All bathroom walls shall receive batt or roll insulation of a thickness equal to the nominal thickness of the wall.

---

34 MOISTURE PROTECTION

ROOFING   All roofing to be standard seal tab fiberglass composition shingles, with manufacturers' 20-year limited warranty, or equal.

FLASHING   Flashing to be 26 gauge galvanized steel where required.

CAULKING AND SEALANTS   All caulk and sealants shall be acrylic latex formulations as manufactured by Dap, or equal.

SKYLIGHTS   Skylights, if required as per the plans, shall be Model DDRA "Sky Window" (sized to follow plans) as manufactured by Wasco, or equal. All skylights shall have anodized bronze trim and insulated glazing.

GUTTERS AND DOWNSPOUTS   Gutters and downspouts shall be located as shown on plans and shall be 5" OG Detail seamless aluminum. Gutters and downspouts shall be prefinished in color to be chosen or approved prior to installation by the Decorator.

Figure 9-1 (cont.)   Sample of standard specifications and procedures

37 DRYWALL

All drywall sheeting to be installed on walls and ceilings shall be ½" x 4' (or 4.5') x 12'. All drywall, including that installed on ceilings, is to be taped, mudded, skimmed and sanded so as to provide an appropriately, smooth surface and finish that is ready to accept paint without any further treatment. No stippling or texturing of drywall is part of this contract.

PROCEDURES FOR DRYWALL CONTRACTORS

1) Costs for normal amounts of touch-up and patching work to be included in Drywall Contractor's bid. Repairs of excessive damage shall be negotiated with the Builder (prior to any such work being done) as extra work. If said work is approved by the Builder then the Drywall Contractor shall be reimbursed accordingly.

2) All drywall shall be touched up after the first coat of paint.

40 CABINETS AND COUNTERTOPS

CABINETS Cabinets are to be manufactured by Marsh Cabinet Co., or equal in price and quality.

Kitchen cabinets are to be white with raised panel design as per Decorator's instructions.

The cabinet supplier is to provide shop drawings for the Builder's approval prior to manufacturing the cabinets.

Provide valence over kitchen sink window.

Hardware to be brass ball in kitchen and white ball in bathrooms.

COUNTERTOPS Plastic laminate tops and backsplash will be provided in the kitchen equal to Wilson Art.

Bath vanities will have cultured marble tops, bowls and 4" backsplashes.

CABINET HARDWARE Hardware to be according to Decorator.

43 FINISH CARPENTRY

TRIM CARPENTRY Cased openings shall be prefabricated openings with standard detail casings applied.

All window casings shall be the same detail casing as applied to the door units.

All bases to be wood, 3½" detail, finger jointed, to receive paint.

Chair rails (if detailed) shall be standard 3¼", finger jointed, one piece chair rails to be confined to those areas shown on plans.

Ceiling moldings, if crown molding is shown, shall be 3⅝" standard crown mold, finger jointed, one piece to receive paint.

Painted quarter round to be installed in all areas where vinyl flooring is installed.

INTERIOR DOORS All interior hinge doors and pocket doors shall be six-panel colonial-style molded door units with standard detail casing applied.

All bi-fold doors shall be molded panel bi-fold door units with standard detail casing applied.

Figure 9-1 (cont.) Sample of standard specifications and procedures

PROCEDURES FOR FINISH CARPENTRY CONTRACTORS

1) Finish Carpenter shall install all interior doors and door hardware as per details including: locksets, latchsets, knobs, door stops, and peepholes (if required); all window hardware; all moldings as per details including: baseboard, crown, quarter round, chair rail, window stools, casings for exterior doors and windows, other cased openings, wood trim for attic access doors, and plumbing access covers, etc.

2) All doors must swing and close properly. All locks and door knobs must operate smoothly.

3) All door stops must be in the correct alignment to allow for their proper operation.

4) Locations and dimensions of all materials must be verified with and approved by Builder prior to their installation.

46 FINISH HARDWARE

HARDWARE   All hardware finishes shall be polished brass. All hardware shall be Dexter, or approved equal.

Bath accessories shall be polished brass and shall include toilet paper holders, decorative towel bars, soap dishes, etc.

Door bumps as required to protect walls (rigid type).

Sash locks as manufactured for double hung windows.

Polished brass kick plate for front door, Dexter #863 4 x 3, or equal.

LOCKS AND KNOBS   All locks and knobs to be polished brass.

Front door handle Dexter "Richmond" Series 516 with polished brass finished and "Corona" ball knob inside trim, or equal.

Dexter deadbolt Series 4000 (single cylinder), or equal, on all exterior doors.

Key lock on patio door, Dexlock Series "Corona" knob style, or equal.

Privacy locks, passage locks and dummy knobs, shall all be Dexter Dexlock Series "Corona" knob style, or equal.

49 PAINTING AND WALLPAPER

PAINTING   All paint colors as per Decorator.

- ■ *Exterior:* All exterior woodwork shall have one coat primer and one coat finish semi-gloss exterior latex paint equal to "Glidden's-Spred House Dura-Satin Finish."

- ■ *Interior:* All interior walls to have one coat primer and one coat finish flat latex paint equal to "Glidden's-Spred Satin."

All interior wood trim will have one coat primer and one coat finish, high gloss oil based paint. All interior doors to be painted same as interior trim.

It is understood by the Painting Contractor that all interior woodwork consisting of window casing, door casing and base will be a different color, to be selected by the Decorator, than the walls.

All ceilings to be painted flat ceiling white over smooth, finished drywall.

Painting Contractor will not be responsible for paint touch-up after occupancy of house by Purchaser.

WALLPAPER   Install as per Decorator instructions.

Figure 9-1 (cont.)   Sample of standard specifications and procedures

52 EXTERIOR FLATWORK AND PAVING

DRIVES, WALKS, PATIOS   All exterior exposed drives, walks and patios shown on plans shall be 4" 3,000 PSI concrete on grade, broom finished, and with ½" x 4" expansion joints as required by codes. The contract as stated for this work includes no provisions for any of the following: reinforcement, vapor barrier, or special color(s).

55 FLOORING

All flooring colors as per Decorator.

CARPET   Carpet is to be installed in all areas except the following: kitchen, master bath, second bath, foyer, washer/dryer room and storage room.

All carpeting shall be Peerless International brand, Style 501 "Just Great," or equal. This carpeting carries a manufacturer's five-year wear warranty and is FHA approved.

Carpet pad shall be 5-density, ½" Re-Bond, FHA approved, manufactured by Bond-a-Foam, Inc., or equal.

VINYL   Vinyl is to be installed in kitchen and washer/dryer room.

Congoleum "Bright Life," or equal.

WOOD FLOORING   Wood flooring to be installed in foyer.

Harco Pattern Plus , or equal. Harco's Pattern Plus is an acrylic impregnated, commercial "C" grade plank hardwood, that's installed directly over subfloors.

PROCEDURES FOR FLOORING CONTRACTORS

1) Vinyl to be cut within ⅛" of wall.
2) Flooring Contractor to patch and/or skim coat underlayment to insure smooth vinyl sheet.
3) Upon completion of work the Flooring Contractor shall replace all doors and doors stops removed.
4) Flooring Contractor to properly stretch all carpet and roll all vinyl.

58 APPLIANCES

All appliances to have black fronts unless otherwise specified.

DISHWASHER   General Electric GSD 640

RANGE/OVEN   General Electric JDP37G, 30" drop in range with porcelain top and black glass door.

MICROWAVE/HOOD   General Electric JVM131

DISPOSAL   General Electric GFC 300R

61 LANDSCAPING

As per Builder.

Figure 9-1 (cont.)   Sample of standard specifications and procedures

protecting themselves from shoddy workmanship. I don't agree. I'd rather work with subs who value their own reputations highly enough that I never have to worry about substandard work. Which would you rather trust: A hundred pages of legal jargon or the self-preservation instincts of a successful businessman?

If we were talking about specs for a big government project, I could see 500 pages of fine print. But we're talking about a simple, single-family residence. If the specs are too detailed, some of the best, most qualified bidders may not respond. Remember, the best subs are also the busiest. They're almost never hard up for work and long-winded specs can come across as a sign of a builder who's lawsuit-happy or just plain difficult. Why take on the grief and risk? Especially if you don't need the work? That's why I keep my specs as short as possible. I skip over many self-evident details and concentrate on those points where a misunderstanding or disagreement may occur. And of course, I also provide the essential lists of materials and work procedures the subs will need to bid the job. If you prefer long, precise specs, that's your right. Don't forget who's in charge. You're the builder and it's your call.

Regardless of the length of the specs, it's always smart to get the subcontractor's signature on the specs for all your jobs. I always follow my own advice on this. Legally this isn't required if the construction contract includes wording that incorporates the specs by reference. For instance, say the contract includes the phrase "per plans and specifications dated {Month}/{Day}/{Year}." Then the specs are understood, in the eyes of the law, to be incorporated into the construction contract. But I still like to have that signature. Let me explain why. Like any other savvy businessman, a contractor, vendor or subcontractor won't want to sign something he hasn't read. So I ask them to sign the specs in the hope that they'll really read them instead of just skimming. No one's looking to win arguments or lawsuits. The goal is simply to promote understanding and to avoid disputes. If you're successful, everybody comes out ahead.

Just the process of getting it down on paper is good relationship therapy. There's no substitute for solving problems *before* they turn into trouble. Having your subs read through the specs should do the trick. This way you flush out all the questions and doubts as well as the differences of opinion before the work begins. Later, after mistakes are made, remedies are usually either too costly or too late. Asking for their signature now (on the specs) can prompt discussion. You can resolve the matter now and reach a truly mutual agreement before signing a contract. Despite all of these precautions, disputes can and do still arise during construction. Should there be a problem later on, you'll be ready. That signed copy of your specs (that you've carefully filed in the project folder) is a much more reliable record than vague recollections of a past conversation.

Questions on the Plans and Specs - Despite your best effort, disputes will probably still arise. Accept it as part of the risk of being a spec builder. When there is a dispute, turn the loss into a gain by learning from the experience. Change your standard spec sheet to cover the problem in the future.

I've never seen a set of plans and specs that answer every possible question. There's always something that's ambiguous or not covered completely. It doesn't matter who drew the plans. When you get calls from bidders trying to work with the plans and specs, I recommend welcoming their questions. Here's why:

■ An interested bidder is likely to be a serious bidder. That's good news. The more serious the bids, the more competitive the bids — the lower your construction costs are likely to be.

■ Other bidders probably have the same question. The sooner you address questions, the sooner the bidding process is finished.

■ Bidders are good plan checkers. More than once they've found a major error or omission that I have overlooked. A memorable example is the time that I sent out plans that included a closet made up of just four solid walls, no door anywhere. Clearly you want to fix this before work begins and you want to notify all the other bidders that may be affected by the change. I recommend that you follow these steps. First, have the architect or designer correct the plans. Second, redate the plans and rename them as "Change One." Third, send copies of the corrected plans to everyone who received the earlier (incorrect) version, and who would be affected by the change.

Awarding the Job

To accept a subcontractor's bid you sign a contract with him for the work. Your local stationer or office supply store probably stocks several different "fill-in-the-blanks" construction contract forms. Some subcontractors have a standard form that they'll want you to use. Personally, I prefer the contract shown in Figure 9-2. It covers all the most important points but is still simple and direct. There's no need for a ten-page contract. Remember, your business relationship with subcontractors should be based on mutual trust and understanding, not on legal technicalities and threats.

The last thing you want to do is to rely on the judicial system to settle disputes or force compliance. Both sides are losers if you have to sue on a construction contract. One side loses a little more and the other side loses a little less, but you both still lose. Even so, I always prefer to have a written agreement that's signed by both parties. It helps you both understand that this is serious business and a business agreement is binding. I strongly recommend that you do the same.

Insurance Coverage?

Be sure all of your subcontractors have workers' compensation and liability insurance for their employees. Your major subs carry their own insurance. They should give you a certificate of insurance, verifying their coverage, before starting work. Your own insurance carrier makes periodic audits and you must be able to show these certificates for each sub. If you can't provide the certificates, your insurer charges you for each employee that's not covered. That cost adds up fast. Workers' comp insurance costs at least 10 percent of payroll for most trades. However, for a higher-risk trade (roofers for example) workers' comp insurance costs as much as 33 percent of payroll.

Some of your smaller subcontractors won't have their own workers' comp or liability coverage. That doesn't mean you can't do business with them. It just means that you need to add what this coverage will cost you to their bid.

HOME BUILDER'S CONSTRUCTION COMPANY
621 Randolph Road
Newport News, VA 23605
(012) 555-6789

CONSTRUCTION CONTRACT

This agreement is made on the date entered below between:

Contractor _____

and Builder _____

Contractor will furnish and install materials required to complete the

(type of work) _____

for the building to be located at _____

in accord with plans identified as _____

for the sum of _____

Contractor further agrees that all labor and workmanship shall be first class, of good quality and in compliance with all applicable building codes. Contractor will repair at Contractor's expense any damage due to Contractor's negligence or Contractor's failure to comply with applicable codes and ordinances.

Contract Documents -- Contractor is familiar with the plans and specifications for this job and agrees that work will be done in accordance with these plans and specifications.

Notice to Proceed -- Contractor agrees to begin work on this job within forty-eight (48) hours after notice is given to begin work thereon. Contractor agrees to perform all work in a timely manner so that Contractor's work does not delay completion of any part of the project.

Licenses, Taxes and Insurance -- Contractor agrees to pay all license fees, obtain workers' compensation and liability insurance and pay all employer taxes as required by law. Contractor will furnish Builder with proof of the required licenses, permits and insurance (including general liability and workers' compensation insurance) before work begins.

Hold Harmless Clause -- Contractor is an independent contractor and assumes liability for injuries or damages suffered or caused by Contractor or Contractor's employees while working on this project. Contractor will indemnify and hold harmless the Builder for any liability or damages for which Contractor or Contractor's employees suffer or cause.

**Correction of
Non Conforming Work --** Contractor agrees that all work will be subject to approval by governmental inspectors. If for any reason government inspectors fail to accept work completed by Contractor, Contractor agrees to make whatever corrections may be necessary to meet government regulations. Corrections made by Contractor shall be at Contractor's expense.

Clean-Up -- Contractor shall remove, at Contractor's expense, all debris and waste which result from Contractor's work on the job. If Contractor fails to remove debris resulting from Contractor's work hereunder, Contractor agrees that Builder may pay to have such debris removed from the premises and withhold the cost of that removal of debris from Contractor's next payment.

Figure 9-2 Sample construction contract

Suppliers -- Contractor will provide Builder with a list of suppliers who will be furnishing materials to the project.

Retainage -- Fifteen percent (15%) of the total amount due shall be withheld from payments due Contractor until the project is completed. This unpaid balance shall be paid when the work has been completed and the contract fully performed and when Contractor has provided evidence that suppliers of Contractor have been paid in full.

Application for Payment -- Payments shall be disbursed to Contractor according to the following schedule:

Amount	Due upon completion of
_____	_____
_____	_____
_____	_____
_____	_____

To claim each of these disbursements, Contractor shall submit to Builder an itemized pay request showing the work completed and the amount due. Pay requests received by the 27th day of any month will be paid by the 10th day of the following month.

_____   _____
Dated   **Dated**

_____   _____
Contractor   **Builder**

_____   _____
Signature   **Signature**

Figure 9-2 (cont.) Sample construction contract

Putting the Pieces Together

As I said earlier, good estimating is in the details. That's our focus for the rest of this chapter, as I guide you through each of the major cost categories on the construction cost breakdown (at the end of Chapter 8).

I won't cover every single item; there are just too many. Besides, my publisher, Craftsman Book Company, offers several good estimating books. You'll find these (and other construction references) listed on the last pages of this manual.

Let's start by looking at the cost breakdown form again. Notice that the first line of each cost category shows *Lot* under unit. This space is where you write in the cost of any work that you chose to subcontract. For some construction categories it's standard operating procedure to subcontract all or most of the work. The main reason for choosing this option? A spec builder saves time and money by hiring a specialist when the job calls for one.

Site Work

Site work includes items like grading, layout and drainage. However, most site work is excavation. Estimating excavation is never easy — for two reasons:

■ First, the calculations involved in finding the volume of an irregular area involve much more math than I for one care to undertake.

■ Second, you can never be sure what you'll find down there.

With enough time and experience, you or I could become good excavation estimators. My advice? Don't bother. The amount of excavation you need on your spec home jobs will usually be small. Go ahead and hire a specialist to do the work. I suggest that you choose an excavation contractor who works by the hour, not by the job. I feel that paying by the hour for excavation work is fair to both of you. Naturally, this assumes that the contractor you hire is motivated, honest and producing every hour. I make a point of being on the job site while this work's in progress. Although I do keep an eye on my excavation sub's productivity, that's not my only reason for being present. I'm also there to deal with questions or problems that arise.

Some builders would argue that I'd reduce my risk by paying a lump sum for the excavation contract. They have a point. But my own experience has shown me that lump sum estimates on this work increase my cost. That's because excavation contractors typically inflate the bid when the job is small. That's a form of insurance for them because they consider small jobs to have higher-than-average uncertainty. That's good business on their part but it's bad business for me. That's why I always pay these contractors by the hour and am around to see that I'm getting my money's worth.

You'll need to have a guesstimate for the excavation cost before work begins. Ask an excavation contractor for a ballpark estimate. Offer to meet the contractor at the site. Have working plans available when you get there. Try to visualize the grading required. An experienced dirt contractor usually can offer both a fairly accurate time estimate and some valuable insight as well.

A grader grading . . .

Excavation Categories - While you're on the job site, be sure to consider all four main categories of grading and earthwork:

1) Site clearing and grubbing

2) Grading for the footings and basement or slab

3) Grading and fill around foundations

4) Final grading for exterior flatwork and paving

Try to visualize a grader out there doing the work. Make a rough mental calculation of how many hours the work will take. Will any soil need to be imported or exported? Are there obstructions such as trees or rocks to be removed or bypassed? How much, if any, demolition work is there? You'll find that your guesstimates get better with every project. However, I also suggest that you simply accept the fact that perfect excavation estimates are as rare as hen's teeth.

Once you've estimated the hours required for site work, multiply the per hour rates charged for the equipment (loader, dump truck, backhoe, etc.). The excavation contractor has these figures. The hourly rates cover equipment and operator.

Good Values in Site Work - Don't be concerned about minor differences in the hourly rate quoted by competing excavation contractors. The real issue is productivity: Are operators motivated and experienced enough to use the equipment to best advantage? There are plenty of ways for any excavation contractor to increase or reduce productivity when working by the hour. Small differences in hourly rates are nothing once work begins. The most important consideration is the relationship you have with your excavation contractor.

Once you've found a competent, trustworthy excavating contractor with the right equipment, use that contractor for all your grading and excavating work. Sometimes you'll only need his services for an hour or two, or perhaps on short notice. A dirt contractor who knows he has all your excavating business is more willing to handle your small jobs.

The rules change, in my opinion, if the site requires a great deal of excavation work. As a rule of thumb, if the excavation cost comes to more than, say, $3,000, I'd seriously consider asking a reliable excavation contractor for a lump sum bid. When the cost gets this high, I think it's best to rely on the professionals These excavation estimators know exactly what they're doing — or at least they should.

Demolition Costs - Back in Chapter 3, I recommended that you consider demolition costs as part of the land cost. If an existing building requires demolition, get a separate bid for that work alone. Your excavation contractor no doubt would be glad to do the demolition — at his usual hourly rate. A demolition specialist, however, works faster and for less, since he'll quote you a lump sum rather than an hourly cost.

Get quotes from several demolition contractors. You want the demolition work done for the lowest price. Quality isn't of much concern here. Just make sure that your demolition contractor is paid up on his workers' comp and liability insurance. Make it clear that you don't want anything buried and that his job's not done until the site is clear of all debris.

Concrete

Concrete Footings - Your concrete estimates should be more accurate than your excavation estimate. The main source of error here is usually in the footings. That's because you won't always be able to accurately predict final grades and ground conditions. Any extra cost for deeper footings isn't likely to amount to much. Anyhow, if you're going to spend a little extra somewhere, I recommend that you spend it on the footings. If spending a few hundred dollars now prevents settling later, you'll save thousands.

Here's the quickest way to estimate footing costs. Begin by finding the footing's volume. Then add 10 percent. That covers most of the likely contingencies.

Some footing subcontractors will quote a linear foot price for footings including layout, excavation, setting bulkheads, batterboards, and pouring the concrete. Usually the price includes labor only. You have to provide all materials at the site. Allow about $100 to cover the cost of bulkhead and batterboard materials.

Reinforcing bars (rebars) are usually priced by the pound. Before you can make an estimate, you'll have to convert linear feet of bar (shown on the plans) into pounds of bar. Use these conversion factors:

Number 3 bars (3/8" diameter) weigh 0.378 pounds per foot

Number 4 bars (4/8" diameter) weigh 0.688 pounds per foot

Number 5 bars (5/8" diameter) weigh 1.043 pounds per foot

Where reinforcing bars join, allow for an overlap equal to 24 diameters. That works out as follows:

Number 3 bars (3/8" diameter), allow 9 inches for overlap

Number 4 bars (4/8" diameter), allow 12 inches for overlap

Number 5 bars (5/8" diameter), allow 15 inches for overlap

Be sure that these overlaps conform to your local building code. Allow about 10 percent extra for overlap and waste in estimates for reinforcing steel.

Crosspieces in the footings should be secured every 6 feet unless the plans or local building code require something else. Use smaller diameter bars for these crosspieces. You can order these bars cut to a length that will leave 4 inches of concrete on each side. Don't forget to include the cost of slag bricks inserted under the bars to keep them off the ground while concrete is being poured. Place slag brick under the bars at a maximum interval of every 6 feet.

Concrete Slabs - If you're building on slab or partial slab, get a per square foot price from a concrete flatwork contractor. The flatwork contractor may or may not be the same as your footing contractor. If you're satisfied with the flatwork job, plan on using that contractor again to do the exterior walks and paving.

The flatwork contractor does any fine grading necessary for the slab. This includes:

■ Smoothing the soil under the slab

■ Digging for grade beams

A concrete bill.

- Spreading crushed rock
- Laying polyethylene sheeting
- Setting rebars for the grade beams
- Installing wire mesh
- Pouring concrete
- Finishing the slab

Make sure you use crushed rock and not slag under the slab. Some types of slag are acidic. That causes any metal (such as conduit or pipes) laid in the slab to corrode. Crushed stone is sold by the ton, not by the cubic yard. One cubic yard of crushed stone weighs about 1.33 tons. To convert cubic feet of crushed stone into tons use this formula:

Volume (in cubic feet) $\div$ 27 x 1.33 = tons

It's easy to figure the quantity of anchor bolts. Generally they're spaced 6 feet on center.

Allow 10 percent for overlap and waste when estimating vapor barrier and wire mesh for slabs.

I figure the actual cost of flatwork at about 10 percent more than the quoted price. Maybe I'm dealing with the wrong contractors, but I've learned by experience that most flatwork jobs include unanticipated extras. The most common extra is more dirt work than expected. Unless things get out of hand, these extras will be small and not worth arguing about.

Most flatwork contractors work on a thin margin. You'll gain an ally by being as fair as you can about payment for extra work. It's tough to anticipate every contingency when you're working with dirt and concrete. Which is more valuable, saving a good working relationship or saving $100? I'd vote for the relationship every time.

Prices for ready-mix concrete won't vary much from one supplier to another. Quality won't vary much either, so I feel that it's safe to go with the cheapest vendor. One note of caution though: Try to use the same concrete supplier on all of your pours. Loyalty is its own reward. By that I mean you're likely to get better service should you need a little something extra someday.

Masonry

Most of your jobs will include at least some concrete block, brick or decorative stone work. Estimate masonry materials separately. Masonry contractors typically furnish only the tools and labor. You get the job of estimating and ordering the materials.

Some masons prefer lime-putty premix. Others like to mix their own on site. If your mason is an on-site putty mixer, estimate eight bags of mason's mix per yard of sand. One yard of sand is sufficient for about 450 blocks or 900 bricks. On the other hand, if your mason prefers premix lime-putty, estimate one cubic yard of mortar mix to lay about 360 blocks or 1,500 bricks.

When I'm estimating block I start with the minimum number needed for foundation walls. Then I add 10 percent to that figure. I make this allowance because I don't yet know the exact depth of the finished footings. I won't know that until the work starts. You can also deal with this wild card when you're ready to order by re-estimating your block quantities after the footings are poured. At this point the results are very accurate. The plans will specify correct block sizes.

Allow for a total of about 50 or so slag bricks depending on the size of the foundation. They're used not only to support the rebar in the foundation but also as fill for gaps in masonry walls. The alternative fill material is cut-down concrete block. That's a waste of perfectly good (and more costly) block.

Don't waste your time trying to estimate quantities for wall ties. Just buy a box or two. The masons will use what they need, and you can save what's left for your next job.

Anchor bolt spacing is shown on the plans. Just scale off the wall perimeter and order accordingly.

If you're working in an active seismic zone or the design requires it, you also need an estimate for Dur-O-Wal quantities. Dur-O-Wal is a type of reinforcing used between block courses and where fill is placed against a wall. It's sold by the linear foot.

Lintels will be required above openings in masonry walls. Lintel lengths depend on the width of the opening. As you do your take-off, note the size for each lintel under section 07050 on the construction cost breakdown form. When you're ordering lintels you'll need to supply this dimension. Noting lintel sizes while doing the take-off saves you time and the chore of remeasuring them later when you're ready to order.

If access doors to the crawl space go as high as the bottom plate, consider spanning the opening with lumber instead of using a concrete or steel lintel.

Scaffolding allows the masons to work on higher walls. Some masonry contractors supply, erect, and dismantle their own scaffolds. But never assume that this is the case. Sometimes you're expected to provide the scaffolding. It's a good idea to settle this matter *before* you select a masonry contractor.

If you'll be responsible for the scaffolding, you need to know how many weeks you'll need it for. An educated guess is the best you can do. Remember that the masons aren't the only trade who'll need the scaffold. It may be needed right up to the time that work's completed on the exterior finish. That's the reason that I like to keep records for scaffold costs in the equipment category instead of in the masonry category.

Concrete Block - Estimate standard 16-inch concrete block by measuring each course in linear feet. Multiply this figure by 0.75. The result is the total quantity of block required. Add 5 to 10 percent to your total to account for average waste and breakage. Block is usually sold in units of 100 pieces. Use the same unit (100) and fractions of it when you do a take-off.

The quotes you get from block suppliers often don't include drayage (transportation) to the job site. When you're gathering quotes for masonry work, don't forget to ask whether the price includes drayage. If it's not included, you'll need a separate estimate for delivery costs. Convert the delivery cost into a per block amount. (Total delivery cost ÷ total number of blocks = delivery cost/block.) Add this to the cost of the block and you can accurately compare quotes of either type.

Let me give you an example. Suppose you need a total of 500 blocks. Bidder 1 quotes you a cost of $95 per 100 blocks *F.O.B. your job site*. Bidder 2, meanwhile, gives you a cost quote of $90 per 100 blocks *F.O.B. the vendor's yard*. In order to compare these two bids you ask Bidder 2 to quote a delivery cost. The price quoted is $50 to deliver the lot, all 500 blocks. Which of these bidders is offering you a better price? To find out you need to figure out how much Bidder 2's delivery charge comes to per 100 blocks. All it takes to find out is a little simple math:

$50 ÷ 5 = $10/100 (delivery charge)

$10/100 + $90/100 = $100/100 (total cost with delivery)

Remember, you can't compare apples and oranges. To find the best quote always make bids as comparable as possible.

Clay Masonry - Brick veneer is installed after the framing is complete. Again, find out what kind of mortar mix your masonry contractor prefers. Then go ahead with your take-off.

I recommend that you estimate brick by the square foot. For standard size bricks, figure on seven bricks per square foot of surface. Then deduct for openings, such as doors and windows. Brick is usually priced in lots of 1,000 units. Once again, be sure to find out whether your brick vendors' cost quotes include drayage. Brick masons normally provide quotes in terms of per 1,000 units installed.

If you need brick lintels, get a quote from your masonry supply yard. You can also have lintels cut from 3½ x 3½-inch right-angle steel.

Brick masonry has to be cleaned after installation. This job can be contracted to a specialist who quotes a price per square foot. To clean brick, all you need is diluted muriatic acid, a stiff brush and elbow grease. If there's someone on your payroll with nothing better to do, broaden their experience by assigning them responsibility for this task.

Fireplaces - I don't install real masonry fireplaces in my spec homes. Most buyers aren't willing to pay for it. Instead, I use fireplace inserts and metal flues. If you use a masonry veneer, don't forget to include the quantity needed. If I'm using brick on the exterior and for a hearth, I try to use the same style in both places. That way I don't have to make a special order. Figure fireplace masonry veneer by the square foot of area covered. If you choose to use a manufactured stone or brick facing, get a quote from a specialty contractor who can provide both materials and labor.

Metal Work

Typical items in this category include structural beams, posts, and occasionally stairs and landings.

This is specialty work so I always subcontract it to a metal fabrication shop. I recommend that you do the same. When you do, be sure that the costs quoted to you include delivery to your job site, installation, and all necessary installation materials.

Rough Carpentry

This cost category covers a great deal of material. You'll find all the materials you're likely to use listed under Section 13 on the construction cost breakdown. I recommend doing your own rough carpentry take-offs. Then ask your lumberyard to quote a cost for the job based on your quantity estimate.

Some lumber dealers do quantity take-offs as a free service when they're asked for a quote. Of course, that means supplying them with a set of plans to work from. This may seem like a great time saver at no cost, but that's not quite true. Relying on a lumber vendor's quantity take-off has one very important disadvantage: it's been my experience that they always overestimate quantities. That's bad for you since it raises construction costs. Sure, the yard takes back the lumber you didn't use — at a price. Most yards charge a restocking fee that's between 10 and 20 percent of the original material cost. Even if your yard doesn't charge a restocking

fee, you won't come out of this smelling like a rose. Why? You still end up holding the bag for any lost, damaged or stolen lumber. There's only one surefire way to avoid having lumber you won't use on your job site. Always do your own rough carpentry materials quantity take-off.

Whether you do your own take-off or the yards do it for you, be certain you know exactly what their quote includes. Remember, unless *all* the vendors quote from *exactly* the same material list, it's difficult to compare prices.

The Rough Carpentry Take-off Process -

Doing a rough carpentry take-off really isn't difficult. Just follow the logical order of construction. Start with the termite shield, followed by the plates, then the joists, the band, next comes the decking and so on. This not only helps you organize the work, it also reduces the chances of omitting something.

I strongly recommend that you use Section 13 of the construction cost breakdown form as your rough carpentry checklist. True, you won't always use every material that's listed there. However, a quick line-by-line review may jog your memory and remind you of something you overlooked. The way I see it, I've got two choices:

1) I can take a few minutes now to double-check my take-off, using Section 13 as my checklist. Or,

2) Skip checking my work and assume that my take-off is perfect. If I'm wrong, chances are good that my estimate is also wrong. Unfortunately, I don't know that, yet. So when construction begins, I'll order materials from the same (wrong) take-off. If I've underordered I'll have to delay construction for as long as it takes to correct my error. On the other hand, if I've overordered, I'm not any better off. I'll be stuck with a lot more material than I can use. My point is this: An error here costs a spec builder time and money. I always double check my take-offs and so should you.

Here are some ground rules to help you get started doing your own rough carpentry take-offs. They apply to most (but not all) jobs.

- If studs are spaced 16 inches on center, figure one stud per linear foot of wall.

- Deduct two studs per window or door opening.

- Figure one 2 x 4 shoulder stud 14 feet long per opening.

- Figure linear feet of utility spruce at this rate: 6 times the number of studs.

- If joists are 16 inches on center, the total number of joists is equal to: floor length (in feet) joist spacing x 0.75 + 1

- Figure construction glue for sheathing at this rate: 10 tubes of glue per 1,000 square feet of installed plywood.

- Figure one 50-pound box of 16-penny nails per 700 square feet of floor area.

- Estimate decking clips for plywood roof decking at the rate of 8 clips per sheet of plywood. Although decking clips may not be required by the code in your area, I recommend using them. They cost very little and will prevent unsightly warping.

Use these as starting estimates. Keep track of your own actual usage and refine these figures.

Lifting equipment, such as a small crane, really speeds up framing work on two-story homes. Have your framing subs include the costs of lifting equipment in their quotes.

Exterior Doors and Windows

These are so easy to figure it's almost child's play. Just count them off of the plans. If there are double windows, add in a bit extra to cover the cost of joining them together with a mullion. This cost is minor, but be sure to include it. Small costs add up. Leave nothing out of your take-offs. Remember, you'll be ordering from the same list. A small cost overlooked can mean a big delay.

Plumbing

This is clearly a subcontract item. Your responsibility as a spec builder is to collect competitive bids from the best qualified specialists, award the contract and spend some time monitoring performance.

HVAC

This is another category that's subcontracted out, and here's a word to the wise: Be certain that your specs say it all. I build in the Southeast. Cooling and dehumidifying systems are essential here, especially during the summer months. A general rule of thumb is to provide one ton of cooling for each 500 to 600 square feet of floor. If your area is hotter and more humid than the Southeast, you may need to adjust the formula a bit.

Electrical

This is yet another major subcontract category. As I mentioned earlier, your main job here is to choose your sub well and then monitor his performance.

Other Specialties

Some specialties just don't fit neatly into one of the major construction cost categories. Here are a few examples of the sort of miscellaneous costs you might come across that may go best in this category.

Ceramic Tile - This material is the traditional choice for floors as well as sink/tub surrounds in baths. In upscale homes it may also be used on countertops in kitchens and baths and on kitchen floors. Ceramic tile remains very popular with home buyers. That makes it an excellent choice for spec builders who are aiming for the "better quality" home market.

Fireplaces - It's not at all hard to argue that fireplaces in modern homes are functionally obsolete. Very few homeowners these days use their fireplace for heating their home. Nevertheless, most buyers still want a fireplace. Whether it's something primal or romantic nostalgia, this is a case where the heart rules. The questions of cost and efficiency rarely enter into the picture.

I prefer to track fireplace costs under specialties (rather than in the masonry section) because I don't install masonry fireplaces in my spec homes. Instead I use fireplace inserts with metal flues. These fireplaces look completely traditional thanks to masonry veneer around the opening. Look for experienced specialists to do the installation work, especially if the material is brick or manufactured stone. Tell all the bidders that their quotes should include materials needed for installation and labor.

Wire Shelving - These days, if you're building a contemporary-style spec home, this type of shelving is virtually a must-have feature. Once again I recommend that you subcontract the work. As always, look for a busy specialist who's carrying a good reputation.

Termite Pretreatment (Soil Poisoning) - This treatment isn't done until *after* the footings are in place and *before* pouring the slab. Termite treatment subcontractors usually give quotes per square foot of area to be treated.

Final Cleanup - I recommend subcontracting this to a professional cleaning service. Most of the ones I've used quote costs per square foot of floor. At this point all I'd do is find out what the standard going rate is for the area and use that figure in this estimate. You have plenty of time before you'll sign a contract for this work. I don't bother with asking for firm bids until after the home is finished. There's nothing to be gained by lining this up in advance, so wait until just before you need the work done.

Insulation

This is another subcontract category. Don't leave any room for a misunderstanding about exactly what work's to be done. Be conscientious about giving your spec sheet to every bidder.

On your next house, for estimating purposes, figure the cost per square foot based on the previous house. Then wait until the house is framed and blacked-in before getting firm bids. That way, the insulation contractor can bid based on actual conditions and probably save you some money.

Moisture Protection

I feel that by getting separate bids on the roofing materials and the roofing labor, I save money. You may not agree. If you're estimating your own roofing materials, start by finding the *exact* size of the area to be roofed. Next, add 10 percent to that area. The result is the total number of square feet of roofing needed. Roofing materials are sold by the square. One square equals 100 square feet. To find the number of squares needed, simply divide the roof area (in square feet) by 100. I order a 50-pound box of roofing nails and then use any leftovers on my next job.

Some roofing material vendors will deliver roofing shingles right on the roof where shingles are needed. Others charge extra for this "prestacking." Obviously, if two vendors quote you the same price and one includes prestacking, you'd choose the supplier who'll lift the shingles. This saves your roofing installer time, and those savings are passed along to you, or they certainly should be. Furthermore, this all but eliminates any cost to you for theft and damage. Damage usually happens during lifting, and it's hardly worth the effort to steal roofing when it's on the roof.

Building codes require waterproofing of foundation walls to keep moisture out of the interior space that's underground. Specialists in this field usually quote prices in linear feet of wall. Be aware that you may be expected to provide some materials: gravel, sand and drain piping, for example. However, the waterproofing contractor normally provides all other needed material.

Gutter and downspout installation is another job for a specialist. Some spec builders I know *never* install gutters and downspouts on their projects. Other spec builders wouldn't think of leaving them out. I'm not tied to either camp. This is another situation where I feel you're better off following the herd. Do all the other homes in the area have gutters and downspouts? If they do, put them on your spec home too.

I will offer one recommendation. If you're putting in gutters and downspouts, seriously consider using aluminum ones. They *never* need repainting. And if you use aluminum gutters and downspouts, here's another tip. Wait until the painting contractor's finished all the exterior work. Then, and only then, should you have the gutters and downspouts installed.

Your sub should provide a splash block for each downspout. However, if yours doesn't, they're easy to pick up from your normal masonry supply yard or a building supply store.

Drywall

I prefer to order my own drywall and let my drywall contractor handle the rest of the materials. Normally that includes nails or screws, tape, drywall compound and the labor.

Here's how to find the amount of drywall you need to order. Find the area, in square feet, of each surface (walls and ceilings) that you'll cover. Add all these areas together for the total. To cover cutting waste add 10 percent to the totaled areas. Take this result and divide it by the area of a single sheet of drywall. Round the result upward to a whole number and that's how many sheets of drywall you order.

Here's a quick way to double-check the total area figure in a drywall estimate. This figure should be about the same as the total floor area multiplied by 3.5.

Cabinets and Countertops

Talk with a cabinet contractor before getting a price on cabinets and countertops. A good cabinet contractor may be able to improve on your designer's cabinet layout. The result should be a cabinet layout that's more efficient and costs less. It's been my experience that there's usually lots of room for improvement. I've yet to meet or work with a home designer who was at all talented when it came to detailing cabinets and countertops. On the other hand, almost every cabinet contractor I've known had an amazing flair for cabinet layout and design. Even if your designer is one in a million and actually produced a good plan for the cabinets, I don't see how a second informed opinion could hurt.

Be sure wall cabinets are hung with screws, not nails. Screws cost no more and offer you better liability protection. That's just in case some fast-talker convinces the jury that all wall cabinets, as a matter of course, ought to be built for safe storage of anvils and lead weights!

Offer to let your cabinet subcontractor know when construction's progressed to the point that he can install the necessary blocking. Blocking is attached to the wall framing and this is what the screws supporting the cabinets are sunk into later on. The time to put in blocking comes after the walls are all framed but before any drywall work is done.

Finish Carpentry and Finish Hardware

Normally, you'll supply all materials, including the hardware, for your finish carpenter. Finish carpentry includes molding, trim, interior doors, interior stairs, and woodwork. Finish hardware includes towel rods, paper holders, locksets, latchsets, as well as any other door or window hardware.

Here's a handy rule of thumb I use to estimate baseboard amounts. First, you find the total floor area in square feet. Then take 40 percent of that figure and you've found how much baseboard you'll need. Here's an example. Let's say you're building a spec home with a total floor area of 1,600 square feet. How many feet of baseboard will you order? The answer is 640 feet, because:

1,600 x 0.40 = 640

Write your finish carpentry specs so that what's included and what's excluded are clearly defined for you and your finish carpentry sub. Most finish carpenters quote costs per square foot of total floor area.

Painting and Wallpaper

Painting contractors usually quote prices for interior work per square foot of floor area. Exterior painting is usually a separately-bid job. When you're first starting to collect subcontract bids on this work, just ask for preliminary estimates. I usually don't ask for firm bids until two or three weeks before the painting is scheduled to start. By waiting, you'll be able to give your painting contractors a real clear idea of exactly what the job involves.

Be sure the painter gives you a turnkey completed price. This kind of cost quote includes all the needed materials and equipment. Don't let yourself get trapped into providing painting equipment. I feel that any paint contractor who doesn't own his own spray rig and ladders isn't qualified to bid on my jobs or yours.

Wallpaper installation cost quotes are usually per yard or per roll and include glue and labor only. The cost of the wallpaper is your responsibility as the spec builder. I recommend that you try to find a wallpaper sub who not only hangs the paper but also picks it up from the vendor. That way, if there's a problem with the paper, the installer will be the first to know — besides saving you a trip and some time.

Exterior Flatwork and Paving

Unless there are changes, or some unusual condition is discovered during construction, you can make a fairly accurate exterior flatwork estimate right from your site plan. I supply the concrete. Estimate labor per square foot or square yard installed. If you decide to use asphalt paving, ask the paving subs for bids that include fine grading, materials and labor.

Flooring

Your vinyl and carpet contractors can bid right off the plans because there shouldn't be any significant changes to the floor plan. Although the cost savings are sure to tempt you, don't try buying flooring material and then hiring someone to install it. This isn't a good idea. In fact, it almost always backfires one way or another. Decide what business you're in. Are you a spec builder or a flooring materials broker? Take a look at the amount of time and energy you'll lose and compare it with what you save on the materials. Don't be penny wise and pound foolish. Have your flooring subs bid on the whole package: all the materials as well as the labor.

Appliances

Set up a contractor account with the local sales reps affiliated with the major appliance manufacturers. Most of the major manufacturers have local salespeople that cater to the contractor market.

Landscaping

Ask a local landscaper to give you a rough estimate based on the site plan. Make sure everyone understands that this is only a rough guess, not a firm quote. Tell them you'll call back for a firm cost quote when the time's right.

Furnishings and Equipment

Personally, I rarely include any furnishings or equipment in my spec homes. The exceptions to that involved specific requests from prospective buyers who were already sold on my spec home.

Salaries, Wages, Fees

You can't always anticipate every fee or swings in labor rates. That's why I think it's a smart move to pencil in a few hundred dollars here just as a hedge against the unexpected.

Equipment Costs

You've accounted for all the major equipment costs that are likely already. However, once again I like to give myself some leeway by setting aside a hundred or two here to cover unforeseen miscellaneous equipment costs.

Utility Costs

I've provided this category as a place for you to enter the costs of temporary utilities such as job phone, electric and water. I recommend allowing a few hundred dollars for each service.

Miscellaneous Job Costs

This is the final catchall category. Use it to list anything that's not already listed or that doesn't clearly fit into one of the established categories. I think you'll agree that my list is pretty long already, so you probably won't often use more than a line or two in this section if you need it at all.

Timing Is Everything

The information we've covered in this chapter and in Chapter 8 should really help you keep your job costs under control and your projects well-organized. I really can't overemphasize how important both cost control and organization are to your success as a spec builder.

Before ending this chapter, I want to add an important warning: Everything we've covered in the last two chapters is paperwork. Now, I'd be the first to argue that it's important paperwork, but that doesn't change the fact that it's just paperwork.

In the final analysis, your profit depends most of all on what happens out on your job site. You're the builder and you're in charge out there. Your main job, your focus, all the way through construction, is coordinating the trades, contractors, crews, vendor's deliveries, and inspectors. Your goal is: *Construction progress as planned.*

As you're about to see, however, your success as a spec builder depends, most of all, on your talent or skill for scheduling. That's the focus of the next chapter.

Chapter 10
The Construction Schedule

You spent the last chapter building your spec home, board by board, on paper. Now you're ready for the big time, the real thing. You can hardly wait, right? Neither can I, to be honest, because *this* is why I'm a spec builder. The process of assembling a home out of raw materials is what it's all about. We spec builders thrive on the flurry of workers, the bustling activity and the smell of fresh sawdust. The growl and clank of a D-4, the whine of power saws and the staccato rhythms of hammers; it's all music to our ears.

Humans are by nature and design builders. After all, why have thumbs if you don't smash them from time to time? Many of us, myself included, find the process of building just as fascinating as the end result. I think that's probably why we always tend to overbuild, going beyond what's absolutely essential for meeting our real, utilitarian needs. Some part of our psyche craves the sense of fulfillment that comes from the act of building. It's probably what draws many of us into the construction business in the first place.

A building site looks like pure chaos, but there's a guiding hand at work — your hand. *You* made it all possible. A thrill of gratification rolls over you like an ocean wave. This is the big payoff for your psyche and it erases all memory of those hours and hours of paperwork. You've focused talent, initiative, skill and willpower on this project for months. Now a new home rises out of the chaos of earth, lumber and sweat.

Time and the Builder, or the Importance of Schedules

You, as a spec builder, have three main concerns at all times: quality, cost and time. From the very first chapter of this manual we've talked about quality and cost again and again. This chapter deals with the last of your three main concerns — time.

Time is different from quality and cost. Time is your adversary. Let me explain. The longer you take to build a spec home, the higher your costs go: for interest payments, temporary utilities, insurance, and taxes. The longer material sits unused on your job site, the higher the odds are of losses: through pilferage, damage or theft. The faster you button up your current project, the sooner you're able to start looking for your next opportunity.

You should also remember that you're not the only one who's affected by any delays on your job site once construction starts. If your project isn't moving forward briskly, at a relentless and methodical pace, your subs will also suffer. By signing a contract with you after bidding the job, a subcontractor agrees to a fixed amount as the payment. That dollar amount doesn't change when delays turn a two-week job into a two-month job. Naturally they'll fulfill their contract with you. However, this is no foundation for a good business relationship. It'll be a very cold day in July before a sub who got mired down on your job site (through no fault of his own) will have any interest in bidding another of your jobs.

Good scheduling makes all the difference in the world. A properly-scheduled job site ticks over with one sub following another like clockwork. Subcontractors arrive with their crews, do their job, depart and are paid for their work. All of this happens without delays or space or work-sequence conflicts. In other words, each sub does the job, unobstructed, in minimal turnaround time. You're happy, all of your subs are happy and they'll be glad to work with you again.

Keep these goals in mind when you schedule work on your projects:

1) Move construction along as fast as possible.

2) Leave yourself *some* leeway.

Number 2 on that list is very important. It's all too easy to set up a schedule so tight that the least little stumble pitches the entire project into confusion like a tumbled house of cards. Control your zeal (for speed) with a healthy dose of realism.

"What do you mean we can't finish on schedule? Do you want history to say Rome wasn't buiilt in a day?!"

On Time and On Budget

Most experienced builders agree that a job finished on time is also likely to finish on budget. Forced to choose between on time and on budget, most spec builders would choose on budget. However, they'd also tell you that it's really difficult to separate the two. On time and on budget are two sides of one coin in our business.

Now, let me explain why that's true. Anything that makes construction take longer is also going to make it cost more. For the moment forget about all the other variables here and just look at the effect on the total amount of interest paid on your construction loan. *Now* you get my drift! Some builders would argue that the converse is equally true. That is: Anything that shortens construction time also means cost savings. This may very well be true. However, it's not something I'd feel comfortable

Construction Category	Completion Date	
	Projected	Actual
Site work	_____	_____
Foundation	_____	_____
Framing inspection	_____	_____
Drywall	_____	_____
Interior carpentry	_____	_____
Interior finish (paint, flooring, etc.)	_____	_____
Final building inspection	_____	_____
Final punch list	_____	_____

Figure 10-1   Simple construction schedule

making a blanket statement about. Mostly because I think it's too easy to interpret that as a license to sacrifice quality for speed.

There is a way to achieve a balance between speed, for cost effectiveness, and quality. Do these two jobs to the very best of your ability.

- Build efficiently

- Schedule effectively

Your biggest responsibility as a spec builder, from here on, is knowing what's to be done, when, and by whom. In the rest of this chapter we'll cover what's required step-by-step.

Levels of Schedules

Construction schedules don't have to be complicated. For instance, Figure 10-1 is an example of a very simple construction schedule. This schedule tracks progress but only on the most basic level. A great deal of information, which most spec builders would consider to be truly vital, is left out of such a simplified schedule.

At the other end of the spectrum are very complete schedules. These list all the details of all the work that has to be done by every trade or sub each day. I've not included an example for two reasons. First, it would go on and on for pages. Second, there wouldn't be any point to it because in my opinion that's clearly overkill when you're building a spec home. Putting together a schedule like that for a small project like a simple single-family home wastes far more time than the schedule could possibly save.

The kind of schedule you really need lies between those two extremes. Figure 10-2 shows my own happy medium for a spec home construction schedule. I feel that this schedule has just the right amount of detail. Use it and you'll always know where you are. At the same time you'll never lose sight of the forest for the trees. Most of the rest of this chapter is an in-depth discussion of my schedule and how to use it to your best advantage.

Scheduling Principles

This construction schedule (Figure 10-2) is a simple, sequential list of tasks. Properly used a schedule is also:

- a set of descriptive, progress goals for the project

- a checklist to remind you of what's coming up next

Follow this schedule and my advice on how to use it and it's very unlikely that you'll overlook anything important, or be unprepared. Check off the tasks as they're finished. Finish the list — and you've finished the project.

Naturally your schedule won't list each hammer blow involved in building your spec home. Many of the steps are obvious. Some jobs get done as a matter of course. They don't require any special attention from you. Any tasks that meet this definition of "obvious" have no place in a construction schedule. The basic list is long enough already. What's to be gained by cluttering it up with pointless, extra details?

Take a moment now to read through the construction schedule. It meets all of my needs on a typical spec home project. Your situation or area, however, may be different in ways that call for you to customize this schedule. Keep this in mind as you read through Figure 10-2. Make a quick note of anything that seems to be missing and carry on reading. When you're done reading, go back to your notes and look at each item. Identify any differences of opinion on the ordering of tasks and eliminate all the tasks that could be called "obvious" and any that belong to a more detailed view than the majority. Take what's left in your notes and customize the basic schedule by simply plugging the new elements in where they belong. There you have it — a custom-fit construction schedule.

You've probably noticed that my schedule doesn't use "start/complete" dates. That's simply because I'm rarely working to meet tight deadlines. If you *are* working under the gun, good scheduling is more critical. Many spec builders find that using projected completion dates as goals helps them to stay focused. You can easily add this data to the construction schedule. At the end of each job item on the schedule, pencil in your estimate for the number of days that job takes. Then just plug in the appropriate start/finish dates on each line.

Instead of dates, I recommend using the following short notation (also known as the *project day* system):

"S" = the date that construction starts

"S + 1" = the following day

"S + 2" = the next day

"S + 3" = the third day after beginning construction

Construction Schedule

Job Name: _____ **Date:** _____

- ☐ Demolition contract
- ☐ Electrical contract
- ☐ Plumbing contract
- ☐ HVAC contract
- ☐ Color scheme from designer
- ☐ Underground utility line locations marked
- ☐ Site clearing
- ☐ Tree removal
- ☐ Grading
- ☐ Soil import/export
- ☐ Job site signs posted (your company, "No Trespassing" & building permit)
- ☐ Temporary toilet
- ☐ Temporary power
- ☐ Temporary water
- ☐ Footing contract
- ☐ Footing materials
- ☐ Building layout
- ☐ Footing excavation soil knockdown
- ☐ Footing inspection
- ☐ Concrete (footings)
- ☐ Termite pretreatment
- ☐ Masonry materials
- ☐ Masonry contract
- ☐ Grading for drainage inside foundation
- ☐ Foundation survey
- ☐ Plumbing, electrical & HVAC slab rough-in
- ☐ Plumbing inspection (slab)
- ☐ Slab materials (rebar, polyethylene membrane, wire mesh, anchor bolts)

- ☐ Slab labor
- ☐ Electrical inspection (slab)
- ☐ Building inspection (slab)
- ☐ Conduit & pipe locations (slab)
- ☐ Concrete (slab)
- ☐ Septic tank system
- ☐ Framing materials
- ☐ Framing contract
- ☐ Exterior doors & windows (supplier holds screens)
- ☐ Exterior door hardware (locks, knobs & stops)
- ☐ Trusses
- ☐ Underlayment bathrooms & kitchen
- ☐ Metal work contract
- ☐ Rough electrical, plumbing & HVAC
- ☐ Water & sewer connections
- ☐ Cable TV rough-in
- ☐ Insulation contract
- ☐ Plumbing inspection (rough)
- ☐ Electrical inspection (rough)
- ☐ Gas inspection (rough)
- ☐ Cabinet blocking
- ☐ Furr downs
- ☐ Access doors for attic & crawl space
- ☐ Plumbing cleanout accessways
- ☐ Landings & walkways bolted
- ☐ Framing inspection
- ☐ Painting contract
- ☐ Roofing materials

Figure 10-2 Construction schedule

Construction Schedule

Job Name: _____

- ☐ Boots
- ☐ Roof vents
- ☐ Roofing contract
- ☐ Drywall delivery (after finishing roof)
- ☐ Brick materials
- ☐ Scaffolding
- ☐ Brick contract
- ☐ Waterproofing contract
- ☐ Waterproofing materials (sand, gravel, plastic pipe)
- ☐ Grading around foundation
- ☐ Drywall contract
- ☐ Drywall cutouts for attic access
- ☐ Drywall cutouts for plumbing access
- ☐ Drywall cutouts for medicine cabinets
- ☐ Floors scraped
- ☐ Attic insulation
- ☐ Flooring contract
- ☐ Underlayment
- ☐ Cabinets contract
- ☐ Ceramic tile contract
- ☐ Finish carpentry materials
- ☐ Interior doors
- ☐ Finish carpentry contract
- ☐ Shutters
- ☐ Dishwasher, range, oven & range hood
- ☐ Finish plumbing, electrical & HVAC

- ☐ Plumbing inspection (final)
- ☐ Electrical inspection (final)
- ☐ Gas inspection (final)
- ☐ Interior painting
- ☐ Wire shelving contract
- ☐ Wallpaper contract
- ☐ Mirrors contract
- ☐ Interior hardware
- ☐ Switch & receptacle plates
- ☐ HVAC vent covers
- ☐ Exterior flatwork & paving
- ☐ Final building survey
- ☐ Landscaping contract
- ☐ Downspouts & gutters contract
- ☐ Carpet & vinyl
- ☐ Cleaning contract
- ☐ Touch-up paint & carpentry
- ☐ Install window screens
- ☐ Polyethylene sheeting in crawl space
- ☐ Final building inspection
- ☐ Temporary power (terminate service)
- ☐ Temporary-permanent power, water & gas
- ☐ Test mechanical systems
- ☐ Certificate of occupancy
- ☐ Final punch list
- ☐ Temporary toilet (remove)

Figure 10-2 (cont.)   Construction schedule

Here's an example using "S" as the start date. I schedule site clearing and tree removal for day S + 1. Next is grading which I've estimated will take 2 days, so I pencil in S + 2 through S + 3. Now, let's say S happens to be a Friday. Saturday and Sunday aren't included in the count so that makes S + 1 = Monday. On Tuesday it rains too much for the equipment to work. The result is that Wednesday (*not* Tuesday) is S + 2. Numbering work days from the start date really simplifies scheduling and cuts the amount of time you spend on schedule revisions. Remember you won't know the start date and you sure can't predict weather delays.

One more point about the organization of Figure 10-2. It lists work events in *chronological* order. That's not exactly the same as the order of construction. This schedule reflects the order you use when you're thinking about a task to be performed. This can sometimes be very different from the order that applies to actual work performance out on the job site. Here's an example of what I mean. Let's say that your project includes an ornate, hand-carved entry door. This door must be ordered at least two weeks *before* the foundation's poured, even though you can't possibly install it now. But you have to be certain that you *have* the door on hand when the time comes to hang exterior doors.

The Perfect Schedule?

Let me make this crystal clear. There is no such thing as a perfect schedule. Accept that as a fact of life and you'll be a happier spec builder. Beating your head against that wall accomplishes nothing other than wasting time and energy. You might succeed for the moment, but that's all. Chances are better than even that what works this time won't even come close to fitting your next project.

The Construction Schedule - Roll up your sleeves now and get ready to plunge into the schedule. I'll be discussing each of the milestones you pass in the course of building most spec homes. As you read the rest of this section you may find it helpful to have a copy of Figure 10-2 close at hand.

Demolition contract: After closing on the land, arrange for any necessary demolition work as soon as possible. Site planning is easier and less risky if your site's cleared from the start.

Make sure that your demolition subcontractor has liability insurance. Also be certain that you get the sub's signature on a copy of your specs and make it your job to see that those specs include and clearly state the following:

- Old, *buried* footings may be left "*in situ*" (in place) *only* if demolition contractor has the builder's permission to do so in advance. Give your OK if you're sure the old footings won't impede the new construction.

- No other materials or debris of any kind may be buried on the site. This includes but is not limited to wood, paper and roofing materials.

Demolition debris is *not* a proper fill material and is likely to cause uneven settling.

Make it clear to your demolition subcontractor that you're not hiring him to do any site grading. However, you expect to find the site clear of all debris and free of hazards at the end of the demolition phase.

I strongly recommend casually dropping in at the job site when demolition work's underway. Any temptation to take the easy way out or to bend the specs just a little bit is nipped in the bud if there's no telling when you might drop by.

Electrical contract, plumbing contract, HVAC contract: Selecting the sub-contractors for these three mechanical trades is your next task. These subs are charged with responsibility for three major systems. The sooner you choose these subs the better. It's safe to wait and select the rest of your subs after construction starts, on an "as-needed" basis. That's not true of the Big Three. Make these important choices now.

Your job site won't be ready for construction to start until temporary power and water service are available on site. Between the three trades there's a great deal of rough installation work to complete before you call for the framing inspection. The need to act on these three choices now is even more pressing if you're building on a poured concrete slab. All three trades have pipe or conduit to cut and place within the slab before it's poured. Sign up all three now and you'll save everyone time and headaches later on.

Color scheme from designer: Color designers coordinate the look of the interior and exterior of your spec home. Make sure that you pay your designer a visit early in the project and take a full set of blueprints with you. Color designers need plenty of lead time to make decisions. If this looks like you're putting the cart before the horse, keep reading. It's true we've not said a word about choosing your framing sub. Here's why I'm telling you to hire the color designer now.

1) Remember what I said earlier: Designers need a lot of lead time.

2) You'll need some of the designer's decisions sooner than you may think. Unless your designer starts working now, you won't have that information when you need it.

It's not nice to get caught in a squeeze like that. It means delays and you'll only have yourself to blame. For example, your subcontractor for exterior paint is probably going to want his crews to start work as soon as the framing crews finish. What colors of paint is he supposed to use?

Underground utility lines locations marked: Call your local utility companies and make appointments to have someone come to your job site. They'll send someone to locate and mark the run of their underground lines. It's very important to know where these lines are located before any grading or excavation is done on the site. Your plumbing subcontractor also needs this information to make the required connections to water, gas and sewer lines.

Site clearing, tree removal: Clear the site of anything that's in the way of construction, including trees, brush, rocks and anything else that your plans require to be removed.

Grading, soil import/export: Make it easy on yourself. Clear the site first. On a cleared site it's far easier to visualize the grades you'll need. It's also easier to estimate the amount of soil you'll have to import or export from the site. The best case scenario, for soil import/export, is finding that your site is what's called a "balanced" job. This is a site that requires neither import or export of any soil. That's not the same as a site that needs absolutely no earthwork at all. Sites like that are too rare to bother considering. Rather a balanced site is one with both highs and lows and in the end they cancel one another. In other words, by leveling out the highs you produce all the soil you need for filling in the lows. You'll want to keep soil import/export as limited as possible. Soil is heavy. Whether you're moving soil on or off your site, the cost is high. What should you do if your site seems to call for importing or exporting large amounts of soil? Take another look at your site plan. Pay special attention to the way that the home's positioned on the lot. If adjusting the home's orientation will save you a significant amount of soil import/export, seriously consider making the change. Naturally, like all changes, this one comes at a price, but it might be cheaper in the long run.

You'll need to make some decisions now about the foundation elevations. Remember that these choices are permanent and will affect the home for its entire life span. Take your time. There are many factors to consider, including drainage, pedestrian traffic, and site ingress and egress for vehicles as well as people. Don't overlook your needs, either. Make site access as easy as possible for the heavy equipment, delivery vehicles and people involved in the home's construction.

All the major grading for drainage is done at this point. Areas that will later be covered with concrete flatwork are graded to drain *away* from the home's foundation. The lot as a whole requires grading to direct surface runoff away from the foundation, off of the lot and into the street. The fine-tuning comes later.

Good designers take site drainage into account when they prepare a site plan. Although I trust my designers to do a good job, I also like to check out site drainage for myself. After I've done this I always feel more at ease. You are looking at a big commitment of your time and resources. Does the site plan follow common sense? The best way to find out is to see for yourself. Don't just go take a look. Instead, be prepared to recheck grades and measurements. Arm yourself with a set of plans and a transit level and take your grading contractor along. The two of you are going to go shoot yourselves some grades. While you're there with a transit handy I'd go on and double-check any setbacks, easements or other clearances required by the local building code or zoning laws.

If this seems like a lot of wasted effort, trust me, it's not. If you're satisfied that everything looks like it will work you'll sleep better. Furthermore, it's possible for a simple double-check to save you or your project, usually both, from delay and ruin. Sudden flashes of insight really do happen when you're seeing a project with fresh eyes. Solutions to problems are suddenly as clear as the nose on your face. On the other hand, a problem no one noticed earlier can stick out like a sore thumb after demolition and site clearing. In any event the point is, you can still fix it on paper. This is your last chance. From here on changing the home's orientation will cost you an arm and both legs.

Job site signs posted (your company, ''No Trespassing'' & building permit), temporary toilet, temporary power, temporary water: After the grading is finished and before starting footing excavating, post your company sign on the job site. Everyone, from vendors, subcontractors, suppliers, delivery drivers and tradesmen to inspectors, appreciates the confirmation that your sign provides. That's especially true if you happen to be working in an area where there are many active building sites. If your company sign doesn't list your business phone number already, I highly recommend that you add it. This is some of the cheapest advertising there is. Besides that, it really is productive. A sign like that brings visits and calls from contractors and others who may prove to be good prospects as subcontractors or suppliers later. Keep a record or list of the calls for later reference.

You're already putting up signs so you may as well make a clean sweep at the job. Go ahead and post your building permit. I also like to post at least one "No Trespassing" sign on job sites. The sign provides you and your building materials with some, although not much, legal protection. By prominently posting a "No Trespassing" sign you mark both the site and anything on it as your property.

Order a temporary toilet. Your electrical sub sets up temporary power service to the job site. Then you call the power company and put the electrical service in your name. At the same time your plumbing sub runs pipe to set up the temporary water supply for the job site. Your concrete and block masons are about to arrive on the scene and they have to have a ready water source.

Footing contract, footing materials, building layout, footing excavation soil knockdown, footing inspection: If you plan to build right to the boundary or setback lines, make sure that the corner survey stakes are still in place and undisturbed. If that's not the case, either reset the stakes yourself or arrange to have your surveyor come back and relocate them. Your footing subcontractor can't start work without these reference points.

Meet your footing subcontractor at your job site and have him confirm that all the required materials are on hand. If it looks like rain or if rain's been forecast, hold your footing sub at bay for a while. A good heavy downpour destroys footing trenches in nothing flat. After the concrete pour, rain poses less of a hazard to footings. A moderate amount of rain (post-pour) causes footings no serious damage.

Your contract with the footing sub normally covers laying out the building. However, it's your responsibility to double-check the dimensions and the layout. I can't overstate the importance of getting the layout right. Make just one mistake laying out the footings and you've got trouble. Big, big trouble that just keeps snowballing all the time. Worse yet, your trouble involves officials. Those officials, for starters include the building inspector *and* the zoning commission. Be absolutely certain that your footing layout is perfectly square and completely correct.

How deep the footings go is also very important. Footings must extend well below the frost line on firm, undisturbed soil. Footings that rise from a bed of firm, undisturbed soil rarely have problems with settling. Most footing subcontractors know the soils in their area and know how deep to place footings. If there's any question or difference of opinion, check with the building inspector's office for the official depth to the frost line. In any case, I make it a practice (and advise you also) to be there during the digging and check the depth myself. When in doubt, dig a little deeper. The extra cost is minor, a little more concrete or a few more blocks. Think of it as some very cheap insurance. There are few things a spec builder dreads or loathes more than the prospect of building on a foundation that settles prematurely.

After finishing the foundation excavation, have the backhoe operator knock down the piles of excavated soil. Removing the piles of earth will make life and work on the job site much easier for everyone. This job only takes a few minutes of the backhoe operator's time. Ask your backhoe operator not to spread the soil very far away from the footing excavation. Later on, that soil comes in handy for backfill around the footings and foundation. Naturally, you'll also prefer not to find any of the excavated soil back inside your footing trenches.

Have your footing subcontractor deal with calling for the footing inspection. Your job's to ensure that the building permit's available so that it's signed off when the inspection's complete.

Concrete (footings), termite pretreatment, masonry materials, masonry contract, grading for drainage inside foundation: Take delivery of the concrete block if possible the day after the pour is done for the footings. With a little luck, your block mason is ready and waiting with his crew to descend on the job site.

As a spec builder, your main task at this stage is to do everything in your power to prevent any delay. I've found that open footings have an uncanny, almost magnetic, attraction for both children and rain. Luckily, footings lose their allure shortly after the block masons set to work. I always breath a little easier when the footings have a course or two of block work on top of them.

If you're not building on a poured concrete slab foundation, arrange for termite pretreatment now.

As the work on the foundation progresses make some comparisons between its final elevation and the finish grades of any walkways, landings, steps and parking areas. Moisture must be prevented from collecting next to any wood framing or siding. To accomplish this, be sure that the completed foundation extends at least 6 inches above the height of all other finish grades. Also be sure you allow for a minimum clearance of 2 feet between the finish grade and the bottom of the floor joists. If you happen to be building with piers, make sure they're ½ inch shorter than the outside of the walls.

In my area (the Southeast), we sometimes use a masonry foundation with a home built on a concrete slab. In that case, we top out the foundation with form block instead of solid cap block. No matter what type of foundation you use, it's important to check the finish grade against the height of the foundation.

Be sure the crawl space has adequate ventilation. Typically, concrete block foundations are ventilated by turning a block sideways at the appropriate interval. Check this spacing against the local building code requirements.

The top course of a concrete block foundation includes the anchor bolts. These bolts attach the bottom plate (and the building) to the foundation.

After the block masons finish the foundation surrounding the crawl space, grade the soil inside so puddling in wet weather won't be a problem. Slope the soil toward some point where water can exit the crawl space, such as an opening for an access door.

This is a job that's far quicker and easier if it's done now. Don't leave it for later because once the framing crews start work it really will be a *crawl* space. If there's not a ready-made outlet for water drainage out of the crawl space, drill or knock a few holes in the block at ground level to allow excess water to escape.

Foundation survey: Many construction lenders require a foundation survey once the foundation's complete. The lender wants independent confirmation that the home is properly sited as intended. The inspections that you've personally made are the best guarantee that your lender's surveyor won't find any problems.

What if it turns out that the footings are seriously out of place? Well to begin with, your project is off to a *very* bad start. As I see it, you can do one of two things at this point and still salvage something:

1) Try to keep the work that's already done from being a total loss. Correct the problems you can, as completely as possible. However, be aware you'll have to be quick and really scramble.

2) Start construction over again from zero. This time, however, get it right!

If you inspect the initial building layout yourself, however, the foundations can't help but be square and right where they belong. If your site presents unusual layout problems, I'd think seriously about hiring a professional surveyor for the layout.

Plumbing, electrical and HVAC slab rough-in, plumbing inspection (slab): After the block masons complete the foundation, backfill around the foundation's inside perimeter. Make a point of seeing that the backfill gets tamped down thoroughly. This helps prevent settling problems later on. As they excavate their trench lines, different subs are bound to produce some excess soil. This soil works fine as fill and if you need more fill than the site provides, here's an economical solution. I use some of the same crushed rock that will make the base under the slab. Before you use any rock for fill, however, make sure that all of the under-slab plumbing, electrical and HVAC pipes and conduit lines are in place. Digging a trench through rock fill makes quite a mess of things.

Be sure your plumbing subcontractor's trenches for the sewer lines are deep enough so that the pipes rest in stable soil. The second worst disaster for a home (a settling foundation takes first prize) is having a break in the sewer line somewhere under the foundation slab. The same kind of break in a water line takes third prize, so the same caution applies to those trenches.

One of your plumbing subcontractor's duties is calling for the rough plumbing inspection before any of the supply or waste lines are covered.

Slab materials: (rebar, polyethylene membrane, wire mesh, anchor bolts), slab labor, electrical inspection (slab), building inspection (slab): After you've had the slab area graded, arrange a site walk-through with your concrete subcontractor. You want to put the burden of identifying problems before work begins on the sub's shoulders. All of the necessary materials should be immediately available and already on site. Your concrete sub's also responsible for calling for the slab inspection when work is complete. Your contract with this sub effectively makes him (not you) the one who's accountable to the inspector.

Conduit & pipe locations (slab), concrete (slab): Never pour concrete for a slab without first checking (measuring) where conduit and pipes have been located to emerge from the slab. It's too late to make any changes after you pour the concrete. Don't allow chance to play any part in the position of pipe or conduit that comes up through the slab. An ounce of diligence now saves pounds of trouble later.

Septic tank system: If there's to be a septic tank system, put it in before you take delivery of the framing materials. The excavation equipment for the installation

needs room to work in as well as easy access to the right location on the job site. Storing lumber takes up a great deal of available space on *any* job site. Once your job site's littered with framing crews and materials it's difficult or downright impossible to arrange the amount of open space needed. If you're working on a small site, the problems are insurmountable. Besides, it's in your best interests to finish all the dirt work as soon as possible. When you know there won't be any more delays due to rain, that's one more worry off your back. Anyhow, the dirt disturbed and replaced in this process needs plenty of time to settle before any landscaping is done. Furthermore, once the septic tank's in, your plumbing sub can finish the last exterior plumbing task. That's the connection of the home's drain to the septic system. One special caution here: Clearly rope off the area over the drain field lines. The last thing you want is for someone to excavate or run heavy equipment over the field lines or septic tank.

Framing materials, framing contract: Order framing materials using your take-off sheets. Stagger the delivery of the framing materials. Too much material on the site at any one time obstructs everyone's progress. Furthermore, it seems to promote losses to damage and theft. Be sure your framing sub and crews are in line to start work within a day or two of the first material delivery. Be sure not to forget the following materials in your first delivery:

- lumber for plates
- termite barrier materials
- moisture barrier materials

During framing, stay close to the action. Keep ahead of the framer with the ordering and delivery to the site of framing materials. Work closely with your contact at the lumberyard. If you can, arrange to deal with a yard that sends a salesman out to your site on a regular basis when the framers are working. Make a point of communicating with your framing sub. Are the deliveries adequate and properly timed to the framing crew's work pace? Experienced, motivated framers roar through materials at truly alarming rates. That's something I not only encourage, but also do all I can to aid and abet. Time is money.

When I have more than one house under construction, I authorize a laborer to sign for deliveries when I'm unavailable. This laborer's primary responsibility is to hump materials, clean up around the site during the construction, chase down spare parts and run errands — basically anything that doesn't require a skilled

tradesman. When something is needed in a hurry, your laborer can make a quick run to the supply store. Work is easier for all trades when the building and site are free of debris and materials are kept neat and organized. Your subs can work better and everyone can see what's going on. Material and equipment kept neat and tidy maximize production and minimize damage and loss.

Exterior doors & windows (supplier holds screens), exterior door hardware (locks, knobs & stops): Don't take delivery of exterior doors and windows until they're needed. Chances are better than good they'll either be stolen or damaged should they sit around on the job site for even a few days, let alone weeks. Make arrangements with your window supplier for the screens to be held at his supply house until you call for them. Most supply houses are glad to accommodate you on this request. Wait to take delivery of the window screens until the home's nearly finished. ("Install window screens" appears near the end of the second page of Figure 10-2.)

Check for yourself that exterior doors are correctly installed. Many rough framers feel they've done their bit by nailing doors up double quick. They leave the fine tuning to the finish carpenter. In my opinion that attitude means trouble. Take a look at Figure 9-1, starting on page 145 back in Chapter 9. The sample specifications for rough carpentry include a section with the heading *Procedures for Framing Contractors.* Item number 7 places responsibility for the proper installation of exterior doors squarely on the framing sub's shoulders. Be certain your framing sub understands this and agrees completely.

Make certain that the exterior doors hang plumb and swing freely *before* any drywall goes up. It's far more difficult and costly to make these adjustments *after* the drywall's up. Let me explain why. As crews hang drywall they often butt it to door frames, effectively locking them in place. If a door is out of plumb, fixing it takes more time and uses tools and techniques more suited to a demolition job. Just getting the door hung correctly isn't the end of the problem because there's sure to be at least some drywall damage to repair.

Your framing sub is also responsible for installing the blocking that secures the door frames. An exterior door should *never* be hung exclusively from the surrounding trim. Always drive at least one long screw per hinge through the door frame, the blocking and then into the framing. The last step is to check the weatherstripping for gaps. There shouldn't be any, if the framers installed the door correctly and in plumb.

Installation of locksets and knobs is one of your framing subcontractor's jobs. It ensures, first of all, the doors work properly and, second, allows you to secure the house. As soon as the drywall is hung, install a door stop for each exterior door. This bumper keeps the door knob from punching a hole in the drywall every time the door's opened too wide.

Order materials with more than usual care as the framing nears completion. I recommend arranging a meeting with your framing subcontractor at this point. At this meeting estimate what's needed in order to finish the job.

Trusses: If you use them, order trusses as soon as the foundation's finished. That way you guarantee that the trusses will be ready and waiting for your framer to use. Your truss installer can *bid* from the plans. However, be certain working measurements come from the actual building. If these measurements are different from those shown on the plans, the truss manufacturer will have to make adjustments.

Underlayment bathrooms & kitchen: Install underlayment, such as particleboard or plywood, in all of the vinyl flooring areas. The underlayment serves several purposes:

- gives the floor a more solid feel

- reduces sound transmission

- provides a smooth, regular base for the adhesive and later the vinyl

No matter what kind of underlayment you use, be sure to let your plumbing subcontractor know how thick it is. The DWV pipes, particularly for toilet drains, must be extended to match the underlayment's thickness.

I prefer to deal with this by having my framing sub install the underlayment immediately after framing and sheathing are completed. That way, the underpayment is already in place before the plumbing sub starts work. I've found a *fait accompli* (done deed) is usually a very effective communicator.

Metal work contract: Now that framing's begun, it's time to get firm bids on any metal fabrication work. At this stage the bidders can see just what's needed and take their measurements right off of the building.

Rough electrical, plumbing & HVAC: When the framing crews move up to start on the second floor, be prepared for rough electrical, plumbing and HVAC crews to start work. Also make yourself available for the inevitable questions. Be ready to settle conflicts as they arise. Walk through the house with each of these subs before they begin work. Point out any omissions, inconsistencies, or changes. Carry a set of working drawings with you. Your primary focus will be on the location of fixtures, receptacles, outlets, valves, etc.

How these tradesmen run their lines to where they're needed is their business. You won't have time to do your job if you don't let them do their jobs. Simply make it clear that the same standards apply for everyone. You specifically do not want any:

1) Structural problems

2) Building code problems or violations

3) Pipes, conduit or equipment exposed in incorrect locations

4) Conflicts arising between trades

Try to head off conflict by identifying problems and dealing with them ahead of time. If subs who'll be working on the site at the same time don't know one another already, make a point of introducing them. Speaking for myself, I prefer my subs to work out any conflict among themselves. Most difficulties are fairly easy to solve once everything's out in the open.

Occasionally, however, you'll have to play the role of mediator. My main advice is that you show a preference toward the position of the subcontractor whose work is the *least* flexible. Here's an example. Most of the layout work that your plumbing or HVAC subcontractors do is difficult or expensive to change or reroute. In other words, it's inflexible. In comparison, the layout work done by your electrical sub is extremely flexible. An electrical sub rarely, if ever, finds it any trouble at all to work around either the plumbing or HVAC layouts. I suggest that you follow my practice of giving both the HVAC and the plumbing sub a head start on the electrical sub when it's time for all three to start doing layout.

In any case, make it a habit to check all the work on your job site. Don't assume that every sub knows exactly what has to be done and therefore will keep the work moving along smoothly. Universal contentment is a rare state in human affairs. A construction site's no exception. The moment you think you've got it all under control — that's the moment to check your back and see what's about to pounce on you from behind. Remind yourself regularly that your job is coordinating and managing the flow of work.

Water & sewer connections: Rough plumbing includes running water and sewer service lines from the public sewer and water main to the home. Your plumbing subcontractor may want to put off running these lines. Don't allow this to happen! If your plumbing sub delays the hookups, it's inevitable that you'll wait for hookups later.

Here are just a few good reasons why it's in your best interests to see that the hookups are put in during the rough plumbing phase:

1) The plumbing sub is already on the site and working. Doing hookups now means the plumbing sub won't need to come back to your job site until it's time for trim-out work and installation of the plumbing fixtures.

2) With the hookups complete you can schedule the final grading.

3) Running hookups now will allow the soil fill in the trenches that much more time to settle before landscaping.

4) The septic system, if used, is already in place. Running the utility hookups now amounts to the last bit of serious dirt work, except for the finish grading that comes right afterward.

So why not get it done and off your mind?

Cable TV rough-in: If it's customary in your area to provide the wiring for cable television hookup, arrange to have the rough-in work done now.

Insulation contract: Hold off collecting firm bids for the insulation work until framing is complete, or nearly so, and the roof decking is complete. Bidders can turn in more precise estimates at this point.

I've always scheduled insulation installation before calling for the framing inspection. The building inspectors in my area haven't ever objected to this practice. However, that's not always the case. Spec builders in other regions tell me that building inspectors in some areas insist on inspecting the framing *before* insulation goes up. If you're not sure what your building inspectors prefer, call them and find out now.

Plumbing inspection (rough), electrical inspection (rough), gas inspection (rough): Tell all of these subcontractors that you expect them to call for inspections immediately upon completing their work. Be forewarned, some of your subs won't be exactly conscientious about this duty. However, any sub is quickly prodded into action with the threat of withholding their payment until their work passes inspection.

In all cases (this is a rare but genuine absolute) it's best to get all inspections over and done just as soon as possible. If a change or addition is required by the inspector, the sooner you know about it, the sooner you can deal with the problem and move ahead.

Building inspectors are government employees. Most of them have the advantage of generous paid vacations, paid holidays and paid sick leave. Take this into consideration in scheduling your inspections. Let's say you need an inspection done. However, the inspector has the day off or has different priorities than you do. Guess who wins this contest? That's right, you get to sit on your busy little beehive of a building site and wait. This really isn't your sub's problem; it's your problem. However, a delay in an inspection is a delay and a loss for both you and the sub. Your best defense against delayed inspections is a good offense. Call for inspections as soon as possible and urge all of your subs to do the same.

In many smaller communities, a single inspector is the entire office and acts as a jack-of-all-trades, performing almost all of the inspections. This is both an advantage and a disadvantage from your point of view. As a spec builder the biggest disadvantage to working with just one inspector is simply that if the inspector's not in, you're out of luck. Period. You, the project, and everyone involved can't do anything but wait. How long? Whatever it takes. That's a big disadvantage. However, here are two advantages to the same situation, one inspector doing all the inspections:

1) This inspector, over time, tends to become a member of *your* team. Taking on the role of a wise, consistent advisor. Ready to offer sage and prudent counsel whenever a problem arises.

2) Building codes all leave some room for interpretation. Something that one inspector approves or chooses not to question, another may very well challenge or cite as a violation. Just as too many cooks spoil the broth — too many inspectors' opinions put you behind schedule.

Inspectors can help you in several other ways as well. Say, for example, your budget doesn't allow you the luxury of paying an engineer to be on the job site. The inspector can help you avoid many common engineering problems. Lastly, the inspector makes a handy whipping boy. That's especially true when you have to cajole your subs to do things the right way, instead of the easy way. "Gee guys, you know I'm on your side. Doing the work over isn't something that makes me

You really can't fight city hall ...

happy either. But my hands are tied. I've done all I can. This time the inspector says we have to do it by the book or it's a 'no go,' and he means it. He's not going to sign us off with anything less.''

Furthermore, you do need someone to act as your quality control. An outsider is often the best person for this job and building inspectors really are the construction industry's quality control managers. They provide this service to your whole area and do so for the cost of a building permit. Keep this in mind and approach building inspectors accordingly. Don't look upon building inspectors as adversaries. Instead, think of them as allies and team mates.

By the way, there's absolutely nothing to be gained by becoming visibly upset with a building inspector. You're the only one who loses if you draw battle lines or make threats. All that a show of temper does is sow the seeds of ill will and hostility throughout the job site.

Mind you, I haven't always been able to follow my own good advice. At the same time, I've also never, not even once, won an argument with an inspector. Neither will you. That's the way the system works. Live with it or get out now. Show your professionalism by smoothly blending in with it.

Cabinet blocking, furr downs, access doors for attic & crawl space, plumbing cleanout accessways, landings & walkways bolted: Double-check all of these items after all of the framing is finished. Check to be certain that the mechanical trades passed the first round of inspections and these are properly signed off on your building permit. You're closing in on a big milestone — the framing inspection. Let's run through the last minute checks and tasks now. We'll start with a quick checklist:

- access entries and medicine cabinet openings framed

- medicine cabinets centered over vanities (not over plumbing fixtures)

- all bathroom and kitchen blocking in

- all exterior walkways or decks securely bolted to the joists between floors

You may find the data in Figure 10-3 helpful at this stage. It lists measurements for common finish carpentry items found in most kitchens, bathrooms and closets.

When your finish carpentry subcontractor arrives on the job site, hanging cabinets and installing hardware is the first order of business. Do yourself and this sub a favor now before you call for the framing inspection. Mark the locations of the blocking. Obviously you must do so *before* the drywall crews start work, since the drywall completely hides blocking. Before hanging drywall, however, it's easy to leave a sign making blocks easy to locate later. Here's how I mark my blocks. I take a lumber-marking crayon with me and take a tour through the building. I'm looking for blocks and at each one I mark the floor near the wall and directly below

Kitchen

Stove, width	21" - 30"
Range hood, width	24" - 30"
Space for refrigerator, width	33"
Refrigerator, width	28"
Kitchen countertop, height	36"
Kitchen cabinets, height (measured from base)	54"
Built-in table top, height	27"
Double sink, width	33"

Balcony, stairs, landing, doors

Balcony, width	4'6"
Stairs, width	44"
Stair handrails, height (above stair nose)	34" - 38"
Guardrails, height	42"
Peep hole, height	56"

Closets

Closet rod, height	63"
Closet shelf, height	68"
Water heater, height (minimum clearance, when installed under HVAC unit)	38"

Bathroom

Lavatory cabinet, height	32"
Towel rod, height (in tub)	68"
Towel rod, height (over commode)	52"
Shower curtain rod, height	78"
Medicine cabinet, height (measured from bottom edge of rough cut opening)	54"
Toilet paper holder, height (minimum)	17"

Figure 10-3   Common height and width measurements

the center of the block. Bring on the drywallers! I know exactly where the blocking is and my finish carpentry sub or cabinet installer will too. Providing them with a road map for these cabinet supports really makes their job much easier.

Framing inspection: This is a really big step. Fail this inspection and construction stops dead in its tracks. Pass it and that cloud of anxiety disappears and building goes right on marching toward completion as scheduled.

Before calling for the framing inspection, clean up both the building and your job site. Now that you're not peering over and around heaps of scrap or disorderly piles of materials you can take a really good look around. Here are a few more reasons to do a good cleaning up now:

■ A clean job site makes a better impression on the inspector.

■ A clean job site makes the inspector's job quicker and easier.

■ The floors have to be cleared of debris before the drywall crews start work, so you're going to have to do it anyway. You may as well do it now.

Imagine yourself discovering a major oversight at the very same moment as the framing inspector. Not a pretty picture is it? For your own peace of mind, and a good night's sleep before the framing inspection, do a dry-run framing inspection of your own. Are you satisfied that everything is as it should be? Do you feel ready to give your drywall subcontractor a green light to start work? If so, you're as ready as you'll ever be for the inspection.

On the day of your framing inspection, be on the job site ready and waiting to meet the inspector. Have the job site copy of the plans with you. Be sure your building permit is on hand. Make sure that all the required prior inspections, plumbing, electrical, and gas inspector (if you use gas), are signed off.

Here are some tips to help you work *with* your building inspector.

- Always be courteous and polite, but don't fawn.

- Don't be evasive.

- Don't try to hide anything.

No one likes to be played for the fool, and building inspectors are no exception. Besides, your inspector's seen all the dodges before. If you're straightforward and honest, the inspector is likely to take a helpful and constructive interest in the project. Should there turn out to be any problems, he's likely to offer you advice on how to solve them, instead of failing the project outright.

Painting contract: OK, you've passed the framing inspection, now you're ready to collect firm bids from painting contractors. Have them meet you at the job site. They can see exactly how big the job is and just what needs to be done. Be available and ready to discuss issues and answer any questions that arise.

Roofing materials, boots, roof vents, roofing contract: Make arrangements to have roofing materials delivered and request firm bids from roofing subcontractors now. As the spec builder you normally provide all of the roofing materials. Meanwhile, your roofing subcontractor provides all of the labor and equipment required.

Arrange with your supplier to have roofing delivered to your job site. Include the provision that the material be prestacked. That is, in groups of material sufficient to complete the work in that immediate area. Your goal here is to minimize the time your roofing sub or his crews spend moving material around on the ground. Don't forget to also order and schedule delivery of any other roofing material you need, like roofing nails, flashing and roof vents.

Make sure that your plumbing sub has provided "boots," or flashing, for all of the vent stacks. Each vent pipe that projects through the roof should have a boot that fits over it. Two different tradesmen, your plumbing sub and your roofing sub, share responsibility for boots. The plumbing sub supplies the boots. The roofing sub installs them. This is an unusual situation that you need to keep tabs on.

I have a standing arrangement with my regular plumbing sub regarding the vent boots. They're always left somewhere obvious on the job site — on the roof, as a matter of fact. I advise you to reach a similar understanding with your plumbing sub.

Boots *can* be installed after the roof is finished. However, it's a practice I don't allow and neither should you. Here's why. Boots rarely leak when they're installed before the roofing.

Drywall delivery (after finishing roof): Now that your home has a roof over its head, it's safe to schedule your drywall delivery. It is possible to take delivery of drywall before the roof's completely finished. However, you'll be taking a risk. At the very least the roofing felt should be down and well secured before you bring in any drywall. What's the risk involved? Say a big thunderstorm comes through after drywall's delivered but before the roof's finished. You could be in big trouble. If the storm lifts the felt any drywall you've stored below may get soaked.

Regardless of when you have your drywall delivered, the important thing is keeping it dry. Store drywall off of the floor to avoid moisture that might collect there. Here's an easy way to do that. Use a couple of scrap 2 x 4s as a base, then stack the drywall on top. If the weather forecast predicts a severe storm, and especially if your roof isn't quite complete, consider wrapping stacks of drywall with polyethylene for extra protection.

Have your drywall supplier unload room-by-room. Each room should have a stack of drywall that's sufficient for all the work in that room. Having the supplier prestack drywall saves your drywall subcontractor a lot of time. Furthermore, prestacking reduces the chances that the floor framing will collapse. Drywall is *very* heavy. Piling *all* the drywall in one room won't necessarily cause the floor to collapse. But that doesn't mean you'll get off scot-free. All that weight may cause a permanent sag in the floor joists.

Here's one last note of caution about keeping your drywall dry. Once the drywall's delivered make sure that all the windows and doors are closed and secured.

Brick materials, scaffolding, brick contract: Schedule your brick delivery next and don't forget to include the wall ties, if they're not already in place. Have your brick supplier unload so the bricks are prestacked for your mason or masonry subcontractor.

If your brick subcontractor doesn't have scaffolding, or doesn't have enough scaffolding, it's up to you to provide it. Make that call now as well and make sure that a reasonable number of walk boards are included in the delivery.

Discuss storage arrangements for the mortar mix with your mason and then arrange to take that delivery as well.

Don't forget the lintels. Remember, you need one for each door, window, or other opening.

When it comes to scheduling brick deliveries, I've found that the best policy is to plan on a minimum of two, depending on the amount of brick needed. Get in a good stock on your first delivery. Then, as the job nears completion, fine tune the amounts more and more on each subsequent delivery. Do your own quantity estimate first. Then discuss it with your brick mason or sub. This isn't a job I leave up to my mason and neither should you. It's always been my experience that when I give a mason the chance to do the ordering they consistently and considerably over-order. Material that you neither need nor use wastes both money and storage space.

Waterproofing contract, waterproofing materials (sand, gravel, plastic pipe): You, as the spec builder, usually provide most of the materials needed for waterproofing. Your waterproofing subcontractor is responsible for providing the labor and the waterproofing compound. Call your waterproofing sub and arrange a meeting at your job site. Talk over the amounts of sand, gravel and drain pipe needed. Your discussion should also cover schedules and the sub's anticipated time for the job. Quotes for waterproofing work are usually per linear foot of wall to be waterproofed.

When the waterproofing is complete, and dry, protect it by placing insulation board against it. This prevents puncturing the waterproofing before and during backfill. Think of the insulation board as leak insurance. Compared to what fixing leaks later will cost, especially after the landscaping is done, the insulation board is dirt cheap.

Grading around foundation: Call your grader operator back to the job site after the framing and the foundation waterproofing jobs are all wrapped up. As I've mentioned above, you want to complete the dirt work as soon as possible, and burying is the best protection there is for a waterproofed foundation.

Drywall contract, drywall cutouts for attic access, drywall cutouts for plumbing access, drywall cutouts for medicine cabinets: Have your drywall subcontractor begin work as soon as the roofer finishes. Arrange a walk-through with your drywall subcontractor before hanging any board. Point out the attic and plumbing access door openings and those for medicine cabinets. Make a mental note of where the electrical switches and outlet boxes are located. Good drywallers won't cover them. However, I'd rather be prepared just in case.

Floors scraped, attic insulation: After the drywall crews are finished, hire a day laborer to come in and scrape the floors smooth. This laborer is given the job of removing the drywall compound, known as "mud," that's been spilt, slopped or dripped on the floors. Any parts of the home where the plans call for vinyl flooring should receive special attention and very thorough cleaning.

When the ceilings below the attic are hung with drywall, the attic's ready for insulating. Use blown insulation in the attic, unless it's floored. If the attic is floored, have the insulation batts tacked between the ceiling joists *before* hanging the drywall.

Flooring contract, underlayment: If you haven't already installed underlayment in the rooms where vinyl floor coverings will be used, have it put in now.

Cabinets contract: Never schedule delivery of cabinets before you can close and lock all exterior doors and windows. Cabinets are very prone to mysterious disappearance, so they should never be delivered before you can secure them. The best protection for you and the cabinets, however, is quick installation. The sooner the cabinets are hung, the safer they are. Schedule your cabinet subcontractor to start the installation the moment that the first cabinet's unloaded.

What sequence should cabinet installation follow? I prefer my cabinet installer to start off with the bathroom vanities. That's because once those cabinets are in, my ceramic tile subcontractor can start work.

Your painting subcontractor, if he's on the ball, can be counted on to ask you for permission to paint the kitchen and bathrooms *before* the cabinets are installed. What's the rush? This sub knows he can save a lot of time by painting these rooms before the cabinets go up. This job order eliminates the time the painters would spend on cut-ins around cabinets. I think any plan that saves time, without sacrificing quality, works to everyone's advantage. If you agree, then go ahead and let your painting sub start work. But when you do also make it perfectly clear that this deal cuts two ways. You'll only agree if he agrees to do any minor touch-up work these areas need after the cabinets are in, as part of the deal. That is, at no cost to you.

Ceramic tile contract: If you're using ceramic tile in the bathrooms, schedule your ceramic tile subcontractor to start work as soon as the vanities are in place.

Finish carpentry materials, interior doors, finish carpentry contract, shutters: Have your finish carpentry subcontractor start by installing the interior doors. You'll kill two birds with one stone this way. First, the doors, which are bulky, are out of the way. Second, the stage is all set now for installing the baseboards.

Your finish carpentry sub's also responsible for installing all molding, trim, and all finish hardware including towel rods and door knobs. This tradesman should also handle installation of shutters and mail boxes, if needed.

If you use shutters, always see that they're painted before they're hung. Never install shutters before the siding has been painted.

Before you buy or install a mail box, always check first with the local Postmaster. In some area there are special regulations and if the mail box doesn't comply, no mail delivery is made until the situation's remedied.

Dishwasher, range, oven & range hood, finish plumbing, electrical & HVAC: After the cabinets are in and the mortar for the ceramic tile work has set, schedule your plumbing sub to come back and trim out the plumbing fixtures. Your electrical and HVAC subcontractors should also be nearing or already beginning their finish work.

Check with your supplier to confirm that appliances such as the dishwasher and range hood are in stock. You need immediate availability and quick delivery.

If your painting sub hasn't finished work, arrange a brief delay with your electrical sub for installation of the lighting fixtures, receptacle and switch plates. Masking tape covers protect the openings during painting. Make a similar arrangement with your HVAC subcontractor to delay installation of vent covers.

Plumbing inspection (final), electrical inspection (final), gas inspection (final): Be sure that all three mechanical trade subs, plumbing, electrical and HVAC, call for their final inspections when their work's done. You can't call for the final building inspection until all other inspections are passed. If there are problems, do everything in your power to see that they're resolved before laying the carpet.

Interior painting: When the exterior painting is finished, your painting sub will want to get on with completing the terms of the contract. Make sure that your finish carpentry sub is all finished. Remove any materials from the home. Have the home swept clean. Now your painting sub can start work.

Wire shelving contract, wallpaper contract, mirrors contract, interior hardware: After all of the interior painting is done, have any wire shelving, interior hardware, and all the mirrors installed, and the wallpaper hung.

Switch & receptacle plates, HVAC vent covers: After the painting is finished, have your electrical sub install receptacle and switch plates and the light fixtures. Have your HVAC subcontractor install the vent covers. Ask these tradesmen to please treat the new paint gently. A little care and consideration on their part will minimize marring and smudging of the fresh paint.

Exterior flatwork & paving: If you haven't started already, get moving with the exterior flatwork and paving now. Be careful not to pour concrete or lay asphalt across property lines.

The art of concrete flatwork and the measure of its quality lies in drainage finesse. Low spots cause water to puddle — if it's cold the water freezes and you'll have ice. Puddling is unattractive and inconvenient, and ice is dangerous. You want your flatwork subcontractor to share and agree with your commitment to providing the best possible drainage.

All stairways must comply with your local building code. Most codes are very precise in setting limits for tread depth and riser height. Be sure all exterior stairs comply with the code. Inspectors *always* check stairs and so should you. Poorly-designed stairways cause accidents.

Final building survey, landscaping contract, downspouts & gutters contract: After your flatwork is in, you can order a final building survey if one is required. Landscape subcontractors won't have any trouble bidding your job at this stage. Collect some bids, award the contract and let this sub get to work.

Attractive landscaping really does add a lot of eye appeal to any home. The cost is relatively minor in comparison with the potential benefit. Allocate whatever financial and design resources you have to spare to this project.

If you're putting in gutters and downspouts, schedule this work to follow the landscaping. Don't forget the splash blocks. Remember to provide for runoff beyond the splash blocks too. Otherwise you may lose some landscaping to erosion.

Carpet and vinyl: Schedule the laying of floor coverings last of all. Never install carpet or vinyl in your spec home before all of the exterior work's complete and the grounds and all flatwork are thoroughly washed down. After installing flooring, make every possible effort to minimize the amount of traffic.

Cleaning contract, touch-up paint & carpentry, window screens, polyethylene sheeting in crawl space: Have the cabinets and windows cleaned. Call your painting sub back for last minute touch-ups. Have your finish carpentry sub install shoe moldings over the vinyl and repair or remedy any carpentry defects. Install window screens after the windows are cleaned. If the home has a crawl space, and if this hasn't been done already, cover the soil with polyethylene sheet. This keeps moisture out of the crawl space and heads off an opportunity for the building inspector to fail you on the final inspection.

Final building inspection: Your final building inspection really ought to be a piece of cake. After all, any major design problems and issues were taken care of before or soon after the framing inspection. However, you still should take this last inspection seriously. You'd be wrong to think of it as merely a formality. Believe me, that's not how the inspector looks at it. So, once more be ready and waiting at the site to meet the building inspector. Be on your best behavior. And be ready to answer questions or take instructions. If you've done your job right you shouldn't need a note pad.

Temporary power (terminate service), temporary-permanent power, water & gas, test mechanical systems: After the final inspection, call the utility companies and arrange shut-off of the temporary power and water services. Then make arrangements to have the temporary/permanent power, water and gas services turned on. Now test all of these to be certain everything works correctly.

Certificate of occupancy: Request a certificate of occupancy now. This way, when your spec home sells, the new owners can move in right away.

Final punch list, temporary toilet (remove): If you've been lucky, your spec home sold before construction was finished. It's time now to take a farewell tour and you may as well combine it with a walk-through inspection for the new owners. Are both parties satisfied that the home's complete? Remember, this home is part of your reputation as a builder and a home's quality is often judged by finish alone. Be prompt about calling the appropriate subcontractors back in to deal with any errors or omissions.

After all construction personnel are off the site, arrange for removal of the temporary toilet.

Chapter 11
Handling the Sale

I hope you can skip this chapter.

If you've been following my advice (and had a little good luck), the spec home you built sold long before you completed construction. If it wasn't your good fortune to have the buyer come looking for you, then it's time for us to get to work.

The Work's Not Over Until the Sale's Made

Compared to what you've been through building a spec home, selling one may seem a simple formality. You may even be thinking of handling this yourself. After all, there's nothing to it. Why should you pay a real estate agent a 5 to 8 percent commission to sell the home you built? You already know what sort of price range is competitive for the home and the area. Then you figure on buying some advertising, not too pricey but with a broad audience. Then you'll just sit back and wait. In no time at all, flocks of qualified buyers, according to your survey, will descend on you, begging to buy. What a racket those real estate agents have going. Nothing to the job, but here they are skimming a fat 5 to 8 percent commission right off the top. And for what? You know what to do. You're almost sure that you do know how to sell real estate. Anyone could do it, right? Right? No problem!

Wrong.

Have you ever actually found any well-paid occupation that's as easy in reality as a real pro makes it look? I haven't either and real estate marketing is no exception. Most of the real estate agents I've worked with *more* than earned their commission. A good real estate agent, and the majority *are* good, provides both seller and buyer with good value for their money. That's just one of the reasons I recommend that you let a professional handle the sale of your spec home. In this chapter I'll go into some more good reasons for you to follow my advice on this. Not that you should need any more persuading!

The Role of the Real Estate Agent

Real estate agents offer you, the spec builder, far more than just potential buyers. Good agents are fierce competitors in the marketplace. They're also avid followers of housing price ups and downs, trends in single-family housing markets, and values. A good agent offers invaluable assistance to you in some, or all, of the following areas:

- finding the right piece of land

- building the right house

- scaring up qualified buyers

- tracking down and arranging financing

- negotiating a sale (The agent, despite the potential to profit via commission on a sale, *is* a relatively "less interested party" than either the builder or a potential buyer.)

Take my advice. Use an agent. Don't try to be one.

Nearly all the agents I've worked with, during my years as a spec builder, did a pretty darned good job. Furthermore, they did the job at what I considered a reasonable cost. I've found that my spec homes really *do* sell faster *and* for higher prices when I list with professional real estate agents.

Why Building and Selling Are Incompatible Careers

I'll say it right now and up front. I'm much better at building homes than I am at selling them. Every spec builder I've ever known has been good at one of these, but just *one*. I've come to believe that's because the two occupations rely on very different mind-sets. I always felt the folks who were better at selling homes than building them had missed their true calling.

Builders control events. (Or at least they ought to be in control.) They control objects, such as brick, mortar and lumber. Construction crews work with autocratic bosses all the time. They also know that without one person in charge, nothing would get done. The end result is that on a job site the builder *is* "the person in charge." The builder points, issues commands and then sits back to watch the orders (at least in theory) carried out. A builder reaches goals using skills for administration and delegation.

Selling is different. It's much more of an exercise in diplomacy. Real estate sales are no different from any other sales transaction in that the seller has little, if any, control. In this relationship the buyer is the one in charge. Buyers know their own mind and they'll make their own choices and decisions their way *and* in their own good time. Your average builder, and I'm including myself here, finds the dynamics of this relationship terribly frustrating. Put yourself in the buyers' shoes. Their indecision and reluctance to commit are normal, reasonable and understandable. For most of us, a home is the biggest single purchase of a lifetime. It's only natural to be cautious. Most builders, however, simply don't have the necessary reserves of patience. Any salesperson knows that impatience gets you nowhere when you're negotiating a sale. The spec builder who insists on do-it-yourself sales rarely comes out ahead. In most cases, the losses in wasted time and extra interest payments on the loan exceed the savings gained by not paying an agent's commission. You're losing a dollar to save yourself fifty cents.

Experienced real estate agents have learned how to deal with human nature. They know that there's only one answer to buyers' chronic vacillation, interminable speculation, and relentless entreaties. The answer is patience. Some real estate agents I know really love and thrive on exactly that type of work. Speaking for myself, I don't. I'm glad to entrust this business to the real estate agent I've chosen. As I've mentioned already, I prefer to work with professionals and I trust them to handle the sale with the skill of a professional.

Five More Reasons to Let a Professional Handle the Sale

I've offered three good reasons for using a real estate agent: First, it's not as easy to do as it looks. Second, agents are good at making sales. Third, you probably aren't. Here are five more good reasons I'm adding to that list.

1) Life is too short as it is. Insist on acting as your own sales staff and you'll pay a substantial personal and financial toll. Don't burn out. Unburden yourself of the responsibility of selling your spec home and you'll live longer and enjoy life more.

2) Spec building is a very specialized business environment. Most buyers expect to negotiate through a buffer of some kind. That makes them more comfortable. When a prospective buyer wrinkles up his nose in distaste at something you worked hard at and thought was a fine piece of work, it can be hard not to get offended. It's better to go through a third party. A real estate agent fills this role perfectly.

3) The buyer is really the one who's paying the commission. That makes you feel better, doesn't it? You can feel free to adjust your asking price so that it covers the real estate agent's commission. You needn't have any moral reservations about it either. You're not taking unfair advantage. The buyer also gains extra advantages by going through a broker. Since the buyer's paying, why shouldn't you cheerfully take advantage of the benefits offered you for free? An agent at work, oiling the gears of negotiation, put the odds that you'll get the best price at better than even.

4) Most home buyers find dealing directly with the home's spec builder very awkward and uncomfortable. They know that he feels personally about it.

5) If you really are better at selling homes than any full-time professional real estate agent you know, get out of construction and get a broker's license!

Enough said! I realize some of you probably are going to try to prove me wrong on this. Go right ahead! More power to you and lots of luck. If you succeed, don't forget what the cost of success was. (See number 1 above.) Then, read this chapter again and do some deep thinking. I recommend you leave sales to the real estate pros. Spend your time planning your next spec home or tying up loose ends and finishing the paperwork on this one.

Selecting Your Agent

Great, you're taking my advice seriously. Now let's look at how to find a good agent, if you haven't already found one. The first step is to go out and meet several real estate agents. Open houses are excellent places for you to start this process. Judge agents primarily in terms of the assistance they're willing and able to provide. Don't put too much faith in your subjective judgment of their sales charisma.

Real estate is a geographic commodity. As a result, all of the better agents in any area will be territorial. Make sure that your agent is active in the area where you're building. Such an agent is a real treasure trove of knowledge that you'll be able to tap. It's like having an informant on the inside with all the latest scoop on where and what's selling the best, including details such as:

- the latest and hottest home designs

- the best neighborhoods for growth

- the area schools and their records

- up-to-the-minute buyer preferences

Just a quick chat, even at an open house, with an agent who's a real mover and shaker in your area could save you days of research.

The listing agreement that you and the agent sign creates a partnership. You share a common goal — the successful and profitable sale of the home. I find that a very comforting thought.

Make sure that your agent is a member of the local real estate board and has access to the MLS (Multiple Listing Service). This is not only a valuable medium for advertising but it's also a very reliable source of information when you're doing market and pricing research.

Cooperation with agents from other firms when dealing with and referring buyers won't be any problem for your agent. Reciprocity is the name of the game in the real estate business. That means the size of your agent's firm isn't a critical yardstick. What really does count? I'd say that the most important traits are the agent's ability, foresight, energy, and your mutual compatibility.

When the Home Is Listed

Regardless of the way you chose to sell your finished spec home, you have one last task to supervise. It's your job to see that the home's in pristine shape from now until you find a buyer. Appearances most certainly *do* matter. Ask your agent to notify you at once should anything need either cleaning or repair.

Here's a sticky little problem that's bound to come up eventually. Your agent has found a prospective buyer. However, the buyer wants some changes made *before* making a firm commitment to buy. My advice is, don't do it unless you've got a firm commitment to buy in the form of a non-refundable deposit that at least covers your out-of-pocket costs and overhead. And even then, I weigh the cost of the change against the likely sorts of trouble and delay involved. Say that you have a firm contract with a qualified buyer. The buyer needs this change. I'd go ahead and make the change, most of the time. However, I'd also consider what being a nice guy will cost me in interest charges and lost opportunities, since I'll have to retain ownership while the changes are in progress.

Once the fate of your spec home passes out of your hands and into those of a real estate agent, despite the trials and tribulations, a vague sense of emptiness and loss will enter your soul and you'll find yourself yearning to be back in the thick of the fray, back in all the action and excitement of building.

Now you have one successful spec home under your belt. Congratulations! That means the next will be much easier. But don't make the mistake of thinking that one success in this business amounts to a lifetime immunization against mistakes and losses. Occasional reversals are a fact of life. No one leads a charmed life in the world of spec building. Learn from all your experiences, both good and bad. Cut your risk whenever you can but don't lose your momentum. Use those checklists. Follow the guidelines I've given you that I had to learn the hard and expensive way. Above all, never lose your enthusiasm! Good luck and good building!

Index

Other Practical References

• National Construction Estimator

Current building costs for residential, commercial, and industrial construction. Estimated prices for every common building material. Manhours, recommended crew, and labor cost for installation. *Includes Estimate Writer, an electronic version of the book on computer disk, with a stand-alone estimating program ---- FREE on 5¼" high density (1.2Mb) disk.* (If your computer can't use high density disks, add $10 for *Estimate Writer* on extra 5¼" 360K disks or 3½" 720K double density disks.) **592 pages, 8½ x 11, $31.50. Revised annually**

• National Building Cost Manual

Square foot costs for residential, commercial, industrial, and farm buildings. Quickly work up a reliable budget estimate based on actual materials and design features, area, shape, wall height, number of floors, and support requirements. Includes all the important variables that can make any building unique from a cost standpoint. **240 pages, 8½ x 11, $18.00. Revised annually**

• Estimating Home Building Costs

Estimate every phase of residential construction from site costs to the profit margin you include in your bid. Shows how to keep track of manhours and make accurate labor cost estimates for footings, foundations, framing and sheathing finishes, electrical, plumbing, and more. Provides and explains sample cost estimate worksheets with complete instructions for each job phase. **320 pages, 5½ x 8½, $17.00**

• Estimating Painting Costs

Here's an accurate step-by-step estimating system, based on easy-to-use manhour tables, for estimating painting costs from simple residential repaints to complicated commercial jobs ---- even heavy industrial and government work. Explains taking field measurements, doing take-offs from plans and specs, predicting productivity, figuring labor and material costs, and overhead and profit. Includes manhour and material tables, plus sample forms and checklists. **448 pages, 8½ x 11, $28.00**

• Handbook of Construction Contracting

Volume 1: Everything you need to know to start and run your construction business; the pros and cons of each type of contracting, the records you'll need to keep, and how to read and understand house plans and specs so you find any problems before the actual work begins. All aspects of construction are covered in detail, including all-weather wood foundations, practical math for the job site, and elementary surveying. **416 pages, 8½ x 11, $24.75**

Volume 2: Everything you need to know to keep your construction business profitable; different methods of estimating, keeping and controlling costs, estimating excavation, concrete, masonry, rough carpentry, roof covering, insulation, doors and windows, exterior finishes, specialty finishes, scheduling work flow, managing workers, advertising and sales, spec building and land development, and selecting the best legal structure for your business. **320 pages, 8½ x 11, $26.75**

• Rough Framing Carpentry

If you'd like to make good money working outdoors as a framer, this is the book for you. Here you'll find shortcuts to laying out studs; speed cutting blocks, trimmers and plates by eye; quickly building and blocking rake walls; installing ceiling backing, ceiling joists, and truss joists; cutting and assembling hip trusses and California fills; arches and drop ceilings ---- all with production line procedures that save you time and help you make more money. Over 100 on-the-job photos of how to do it right and what can go wrong. **304 pages, 8½ x 11, $26.50**

• Wood-Frame House Construction

Step-by-step construction details, from the layout of the outer walls, excavation and formwork, to finish carpentry and painting. Contains all new, clear illustrations and explanations updated for construction in the '90s. Everything you need to know about framing, roofing, siding, interior finishings, floor covering and stairs ---- your complete book of wood-frame homebuilding. **320 pages, 8½ x 11, $19.75. Revised edition**

• Manual of Professional Remodeling

The practical manual of professional remodeling that shows how to evaluate a job so you avoid 30-minute jobs that take all day, what to fix and what to leave alone, and what to watch for in dealing with subcontractors. Includes how to calculate space requirements; repair structural defects; remodel kitchens, baths, walls, ceilings, doors, windows, floors and roofs; install fireplaces and chimneys (including built-ins), skylights, and exterior siding. Includes blank forms, checklists, sample contracts, and proposals you can copy and use. **400 pages, 8½ x 11, $23.75**

• Carpentry Estimating

Simple, clear instructions on how to take off quantities and figure costs for all rough and finish carpentry. Shows how to convert piece prices to MBF prices or linear foot prices, use the extensive manhour tables included to quickly estimate labor costs, and how much overhead and profit to add. All carpentry is covered; floor joists, exterior and interior walls and finishes, ceiling joists and rafters, stairs, trim, windows, doors, and much more. Includes "carpenter's dream" a material-estimating program, at no extra cost. **336 pages, 8½ x 11, $35.50**

• Concrete Construction & Estimating

Explains how to estimate the quantity of labor and materials needed, plan the job, erect fiberglass, steel, or prefabricated forms, install shores and scaffolding, handle the concrete into place, set joints, finish and cure the concrete. Full of practical reference data, cost estimates, and examples. **571 pages, 5½ x 8½, $20.50**

• Estimating Tables for Home Building

Produce accurate estimates for nearly any residence in just minutes. This handy manual has tables you need to find the quantity of materials and labor for most residential construction. Includes overhead and profit, how to develop unit costs for labor and materials, and how to be sure you've considered every cost in the job. **336 pages, 8½ x 11, $21.50**

• Profits in Buying & Renovating Homes

Step-by-step instructions for selecting, repairing, improving, and selling highly profitable "fixer-uppers." Shows which price ranges offer the highest profit-to-investment ratios, which neighborhoods offer the best return, practical directions for repairs, and tips on dealing with buyers, sellers, and real estate agents. Shows you how to determine your profit before you buy, what "bargains" to avoid, and how to make simple, profitable, inexpensive upgrades. **304 pages, 8½ x 11, $19.75**

• Stair Builders Handbook

If you know the floor-to-floor rise, this handbook gives you everything else: number and dimension of treads and risers, total run, correct well hole opening, angle of incline, and quantity of materials and settings for your framing square for over 3,500 code-approved rise and run combinations ---- several for every 1/8-inch interval from a 3 foot to a 12 foot floor-to-floor rise. **416 pages, 5½ x 8½, $15.50**